Sun, Sand & Surf

The Ultimate Guide to Orange County Beaches

Written by Gia Danson-Lucy
and Julianna Danson

Vista Pacifica Publishing Company

Dana Point, California

Credits:

Art Director: Robert Brocke
Editor: Richard J. Collins
Photography: Gia Danson, Julianna Danson,
Peter Phan, Mark Brautigam, Clive Jackman,
Tom Mendivil, Stan Phillips, Moki Tom

Published by Vista Pacifica Publishing Company
P.O. Box 373, Dana Point, California 92629-0373
(949) 395-2878
www.vistapacificapublishing.com

Copyright 2000, 2001, 2003, 2006 by Vista Pacifica Publishing Company.
All rights reserved. No part of this book may be reproduced
in any form, or by any means, electronic or mechanical, including
photocopying, recording, or by information storage and retrieval
systems without permission in writing from the publisher.

Library of Congress Catalog Card Number pfs18328
ISBN-10: 0-9679452-8-3
ISBN-13: 978-0-9679452-8-6
Fourth edition September 2006
Printed in China by Regent Publishing Services

Although the author and publisher have made every effort to insure
the accuracy and completeness of information contained in this book,
we assume no responsibility for errors, inaccuracies, omissions or any
inconsistency herein. Further, we assume no liability for any loss, injury
or inconvenience sustained by any traveler as a result of information or
advice contained in *Sun, Sand & Surf*.

The Lord's lovingkindnesses indeed never cease, For His compassions never fail.

Lamentations 3:22

Table Of Contents

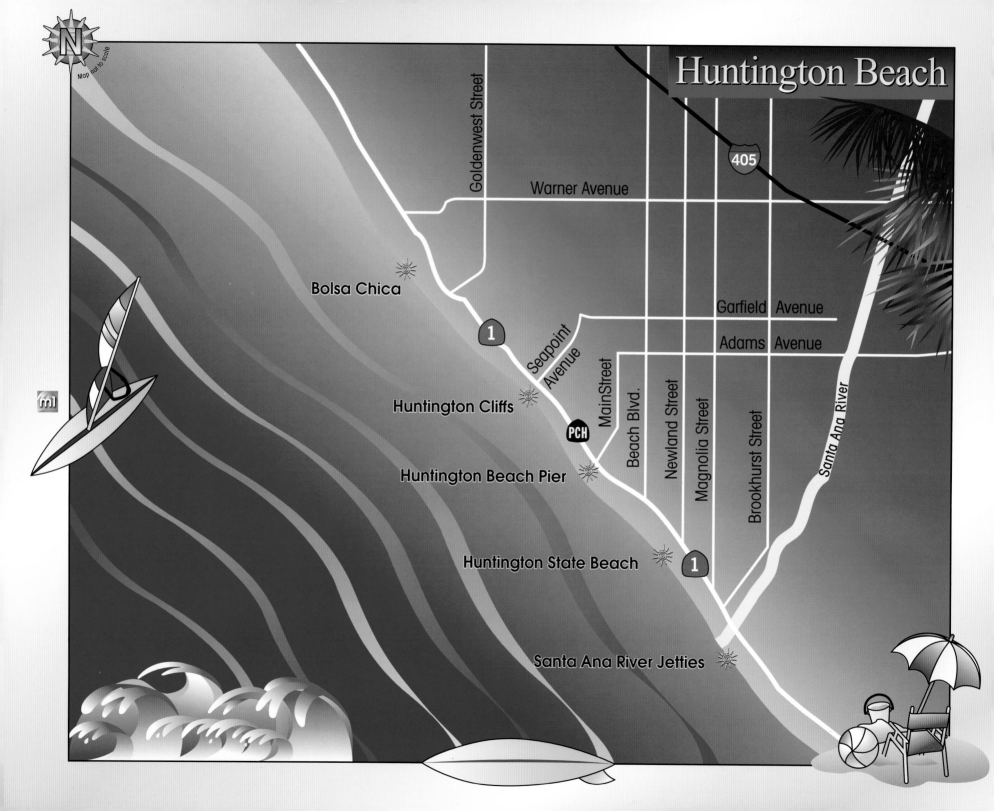

Huntington Beach

Goldenwest Street

405

Warner Avenue

Bolsa Chica

1

Garfield Avenue

Adams Avenue

Seapoint Avenue

Huntington Cliffs

MainStreet

Beach Blvd.

Newland Street

Magnolia Street

Brookhurst Street

Santa Ana River

PCH

Huntington Beach Pier

Huntington State Beach

1

Santa Ana River Jetties

N

Map not to scale

m1

Newport Beach

N
Map not to scale

Santa Ana River

73
John Wayne Airport

55
Newport Blvd.

Back Bay Ecological Reserve

73

Summit St.
Orange St.
1
57th St.

Santa Ana River Jetties
Seashore Drive
PCH

Newport Dunes

Jamboree Rd.

MacArthur Blvd.

32nd St.
Lido Island

Bayside Drive
1

Newport Blvd.

Balboa Island

Newport Pier

Balboa Blvd.
Bay Ave.

15th St.
10th St.
Balboa Pier

Ocean Blvd.

Fernleaf
China Cove

The Wedge

Big Corona

Ocean Blvd.

Marguerite

Poppy

1

Little Corona

10

km2

Corona del Mar

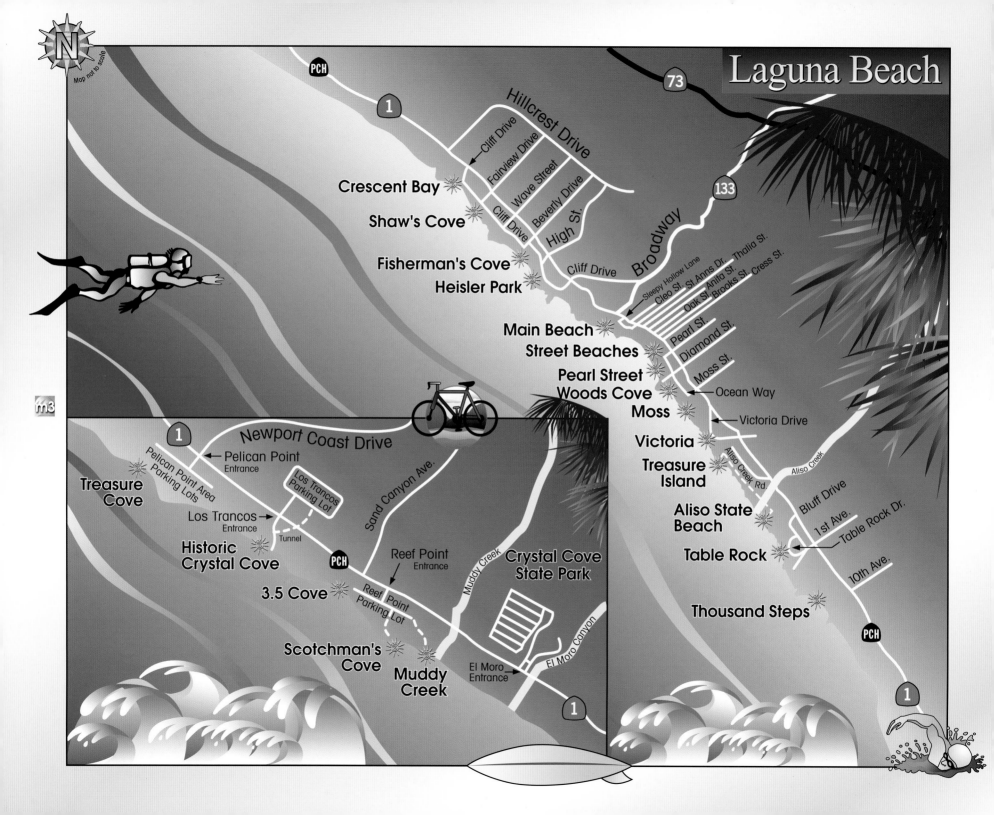

Laguna Beach

N
Map not to scale

PCH
1
73
133

Hillcrest Drive

Cliff Drive
Fairview Drive
Wave Street
Beverly Drive
High St.

Crescent Bay

Shaw's Cove

Cliff Drive

Fisherman's Cove
Heisler Park

Cliff Drive
Broadway

Sleepy Hollow Lane
Cleo St. St. Anns Dr. Thalia St.
Oak St. St. Anita St.
Brooks St. Cress St.

Main Beach
Street Beaches

Pearl St.
Diamond St.
Moss St.

Pearl Street
Woods Cove
Moss

Ocean Way

Victoria Drive

Victoria

Treasure
Island

Aliso Creek Rd.
Aliso Creek

Aliso State
Beach

Bluff Drive
1st Ave.
Table Rock Dr.

Table Rock

10th Ave.

Thousand Steps

PCH
1

m3

Newport Coast Drive

1

Pelican Point
Entrance

Pelican Point Area
Parking Lots

Los Trancos
Parking Lot

Sand Canyon Ave.

Los Trancos
Entrance

Tunnel

Treasure
Cove

Historic
Crystal Cove

PCH

Reef Point
Entrance

3.5 Cove

Reef Point
Parking Lot

Muddy Creek

Crystal Cove
State Park

Scotchman's
Cove

Muddy
Creek

El Moro
Entrance

El Moro Canyon

1

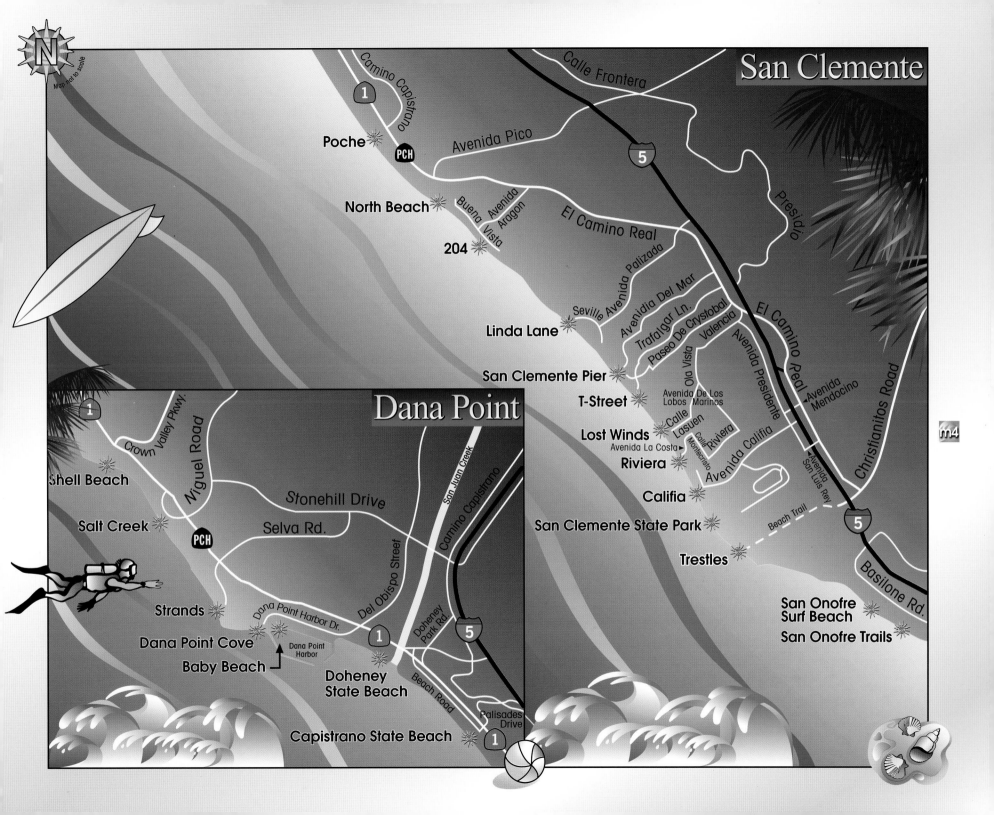

N Map not to scale

San Clemente

Camino Capistrano
Calle Frontera
1
Poche
PCH
Avenida Pico
5
North Beach
Buena Vista
Avenida Aragon
El Camino Real
204
Presidio
Avenida Palizada
Seville Avenida Del Mar
Linda Lane
Avendia Del Mar
Trafalgar Ln.
Paseo De Crystobal
Valencia
Ola Vista
San Clemente Pier
El Camino Real
Avenida Mendocino
T-Street
Avenida De Los
Lobos Marinos
Calle Lasuen
Avenida Presidente
Lost Winds
Calle Riviera
Calle Montecristo
Avenida La Costa
Riviera
Avenida Califia
Avenida San Luis Rey
Christianitos Road
Califia
Beach Trail
San Clemente State Park
5
Trestles
Basilone Rd.
San Onofre
Surf Beach
San Onofre Trails

m4

Dana Point

1
Crown Valley Pkwy.
Niguel Road
Shell Beach
Stonehill Drive
San Juan Creek
Salt Creek
Selva Rd.
PCH
Camino Capistrano
Del Obispo Street
Strands
Dana Point Harbor Dr.
Doheney Park Rd.
5
Dana Point Cove
Dana Point Harbor
1
Baby Beach
Doheney
State Beach
Beach Road
Palisades
Drive
Capistrano State Beach
1

Acknowledgments

To our mother and father, who gave us a joy-filled childhood of days at the beach and instilled in us a passion for the ocean, this book was inspired from those memories. Thank you

We also wish to express special gratitude to our grandfather, mentor and true friend, Richard Collins. His unfailing encouragement continues to give us confidence. Thank you for your editorial suggestions, they demonstrated extraordinary talent and sensitivity.

To Robert Brocke, whose generosity, talent, hard work and friendship proved to be invaluable. Thank you for the beautifully designed cover, maps and illustrations.

To Herb Wettenkamp, your guidance and advice was tremendously helpful. Thank you for the your generosity and constant encouragement.

To Mark Brautigam, Clive Jackman, Tom Mendivil, Peter Phan and Stan Phillips your photographs have helped to make this book beautiful and exciting. We wish you much success in all your future endeavors.

Additionally, we wish to acknowledge the countless individuals-lifeguards, rangers, locals, and organizations-who so graciously shared ideas, information, ride-alongs, and review copies of books.

Preface

The Best Times of Our Lives

We are two sisters with a passion for our local beaches. We seize every opportunity, alone or with our children to enjoy the sun, sand, and surf. Living and growing up along the Orange County Coast, our lives centered around the beach. We found that no two beaches are identical, but rather each beach has its own unique character.

When we were teenagers, we preciously guarded all the discoveries we made, particularly our favorite 'secret' beaches. Sometimes we found ourselves blessedly alone. Today, that is almost impossible.

Presently in our twenties, we realize it will cost us little to share what we have discovered. Now, when we feel tense and troubled we still find that these beaches bring us peace and relaxation, even a renewal. Perhaps they can do the same for you. If so, it will please us to think that we have made a small contribution to others.

We hope this book brings to you readers the delight and even some of the passion for the sea which we still enjoy.

Foreword

Orange County, California is best known for its beautiful beaches and diverse marine life. With average temperatures of 75.4° annually, plus over 42 miles of beaches, 125 miles of bikeways and 200 miles of hiking trails it's no surprise that Orange County attracts over 38 million vacationers each year.

Visitors come from all over the world to sunbathe on white sandy beaches, surf the infamous Wedge, and watch the sun as it sinks over the Pacific Ocean. Sometimes, it seems to us 'regulars' that Orange County may be a little too well known, especially when some of the beaches are picked clean of shells and marine animals. These losses are not due to any evil intent on the part of the visitors but rather a lack of knowledge about the nature of marine life and its frailty. Fortunately, the State of California has set aside certain beaches in Orange County as designated marine life refuges and preserves to help protect wildlife and to give visitors an opportunity to witness the species in their natural environment.

Official signs and rules are posted at the entrance to the marine life refuges. These rules are given in the hope that these beaches can be preserved for future generations. Here, visitors will find pristine tide pools with hermit crabs, sea hares, sea stars, and octopi as well as underwater reefs teeming with fish.

Whether you wish to scuba dive in Laguna Beach, or surf the pounding waves in San Clemente, or simply relax on the shore, this book is designed to help you find the beach of your dreams.

BEACH SAFETY

 Safe Surf Conditions

 Caution

 Dangerous Surf Conditions

No Surfing

Sun, Sand & Surf recommends following the proceeding safety tips when visiting the beach to ensure an accident-free day on the shore and in the water.

- Ask a lifeguard about hazards and concerns before entering the water.
- Swim near a manned lifeguard tower.
- Do not swim alone.
- Never dive head first into the waves.
- Swim at least 100 yards north or south of river outlets.
- Do not swim in the designated surfing area.
- Do not use floatation devices as swimming aides.
- Stay off rocks and tide pool areas during high tides.
- Be aware of rip currents.
- Signal lifeguards if you have difficulties.

Seal Beach
And
Huntington Beach

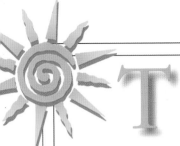

The California Coast is best known for its charming beach towns and world renowned surf breaks. The names of the surf breaks: Half Moon Bay, Mavericks, Trestles, Rincon, The Wedge, not only sound like legends but their reality supports the image of sun-bleached, copper-toned surfers carving up towering tubes of rushing water. But if California has one locale most connected with the beach and surfing it would have to be Huntington Beach.

Coined "Surf City U.S.A." in 1969 by singers Jan and Dean in their song "Surf City", Huntington Beach is archetypical of the California surfing lifestyle.

In 1904 the city founders, Henry E. Huntington and J.V. Vickers envisioned this area as a grand scale seaside resort, a West Coast version of Atlantic City. However, in 1919 this promising vacation spot took a unique turn: Standard Oil leased five hundred acres of the land for exploratory drilling. They found oil. And plenty of it! By 1948 oil derricks filled this coastline. The reality of a West Coast beach resort would be postponed for twenty-six years. Today Huntington Beach is probably just as spectacular as the city founders intended.

Beach bungalows built in the 1970's, along with recently constructed Mediterranean style homes are visually an immaterial background to both Huntington Beach Pier and Main Street; the latter being a bustling promenade which keeps with the "Surf City" theme, featuring the Surfing Walk of Fame (located on the corner of Main Street and the Pacific Coast Highway), outdoor cafes, beach pubs, surf shops and clothing boutiques specializing in eccentric fashions. The International Surfing Museum, a block north of Main Street, offers visitors an in-depth view of the history of surfing and the athletes famous in the sport.

That's the past. If you'd prefer to see surf history in the making, head to Huntington Pier where locals interested in gaining a sponsor, perform daring maneuvers from 'ariel off-the-lips' to 'shooting the pier.' This grand scale of surfing is what sets Huntington Beach apart from other seaside communities. Over twelve million people come to "Surf City" each year. They come to surf tube-shaped waves, sunbathe on broad sands, bike 8.5 miles of beach-side bike trail and watch as amateur and professional athletes compete in surf contests, speedboat races, volleyball, roller hockey, fishing tournaments, kite flying matches and much more. Outdoor concerts at the base of the Pier add to the festive environment. And as an additional bonus, ample parking and easy beach access makes a visit to Huntington Beach nearly effortless.

BEACH KEY

Lifeguard

Swimming

Bodyboarding

Surfing

Skimboarding

Fishing

Volleyball

Bike Trail

Park

Sunbathing

Restaurants

Public Showers

Restrooms

Shopping

Kite Flying

Parking Fee

Seal Beach Pier

BEACH ACCESS: Located along Main Street and Ocean Avenue in Seal Beach. Take the 405 freeway to Seal Beach Boulevard, exit west. Turn north onto the Pacific Coast Highway, then left onto Main Street.
BEACH HOURS: 6:00 A.M. - 10:00 P.M.

Seal Beach Municipal Pier, nestled between Surf City's Huntington Beach and busy metropolitan Long Beach, enchants visitors with its easy-going small town feel, sun-washed strand, and 1,865 foot long wooden fishing pier.

In the 1920's this beach and pier was a place of bath palaces, gambling houses, rum runners and a bathing pavilion with 1,000 changing rooms renting for twenty-five cents a day. Today, these features have long since disappeared, but the beach and pier still maintain an old-fashioned charm.

During the summer the warm weather, sunny skies and bustling beach becomes a picture of summer as families crowd the shores and swim in the ocean. Their beach chairs, umbrellas, shovels, and pails become semi-permanent fixtures on the golden strand and the light breeze, which almost always fans the beach, provides hours of enjoyment for children and parents whose favorite pastime

2a

During the summer the beach and the waves cater mostly to tourists. On the south side of the pier you will find quick, snappy peaks and throngs of day-trippers on bodyboards. It isn't until the fall offshore winds begin to blow and the winter west swells arrive that Seal Beach Pier becomes good for surfing. During these conditions the north side of the pier features clean, ridable barrels.

is kite-flying. At the east end of the beach a playground with swings, slides and a jungle gym is ideal for young children.

Visitors find it easy to spend a day, a week or an entire summer at Seal Beach Pier. Sunbathe, body board, shop along Old Town Main Street, fish or enjoy endless views at Ruby's Diner located at the end of the pier.

BEACH KEY

- Lifeguard
- Surfing
- Swimming
- Bodyboarding
- Windsurfing
- Fishing
- Volleyball
- Bike Trail
- Hike Trail
- Bird Watching
- R.V. Camping
- Snack Bar
- Beach Rentals
- Fire Rings
- Public Showers
- Restrooms
- Visitor Center
- Parking Fee

Bolsa Chica

BEACH ACCESS: Located along the Pacific Coast Highway between Golden West Street and Warner Avenue in Huntington Beach. Take the 405 freeway. Exit Beach Boulevard south. Turn right onto the Pacific Coast Highway. Park in the lot at Warner Avenue.
BEACH HOURS: 6:00 A.M. - 10:00 P.M.
CAMPING RESERVATIONS: 800-444-7275

The name Bolsa Chica, is actually Spanish for 'little pocket' and well named if one adds, 'of sunshine'. As the visitor drives along the Pacific Coast Highway, the cityscape of factories and derricks may be daunting, but this is a transitory experience. In reality, Bolsa Chica State Park and Reserve soon appears and at this moment, the visitor's vision is captivated by one and a half miles of the Pacific Oceans' stunning shoreline on one side, and a three hundred and fifty acre marine estuary on the other.

It isn't only the view which attracts over one million visitors to Bolsa Chica each year. More likely it's the many amenities, coupled with the opportunity to connect with nature. Here, beachgoers can camp overnight in RV campgrounds (water and electric hook-ups available), breakfast on windswept shores, zip along an ocean-view path on bikes and roller-blades, windsurf, bird watch, surf, hike, surf fish, and dine over campfire. And all the while, flocks of birds, California brown pelicans and

seagulls for example, glide gracefully along the sea sailing on warm air currents, south in the winter and north in the summer.

Bolsa Chica lies along the Pacific flyway, the primary route for migrating birds traveling between Alaska and South America. Many of these birds use the Bolsa Chica Marine Estuary (located just across the highway between Warner Street and Golden West) as a stopover to rest and refuel before continuing to their final destinations. Others, such as the blue heron and white pelican live here year round. A wooden footbridge, which places visitors directly over the center of the inner bay, facilitates a closer look at the winter migratory shorebirds and waterfowl such as pintails, western grebes, willets and godwits. Summertime brings in scores of different species including the endangered California least tern and Belding's savannah sparrow.

Perhaps the most interesting time to visit is in the spring when many birds perform courtship rituals. Terns can be seen streaking in, fish in beak, alighting directly in front of a female and presenting her his bounty. Savannah sparrows can be heard singing songs, perched atop pickleweed, defending their territory while trying to 'charm' a mate. For more information just stop by the Interpretive Center, pick up a guide to the birds and plants found at the estuary and proceed on a self-guided tour. Or if you'd prefer, visit on the first Saturday of the month between 9:00 a.m. and 12:00 p.m. and take a docent-led tour of the estuary. Either way, you will discover the secret to Bolsa Chica and why it shines over the urban corner of Huntington Beach.

SURF REPORT

Surfers from nearby surf schools, donned in soggy wetsuits and riding foam learning boards, dominate the break at Bolsa Chica State Beach during the summer. Gentle peaks, packed trough to crest with students, slowly spill right and left and then crumble toward the shore. These mild breaking waves contribute to Bolsa Chica's enormous popularity among beginning surfers.

After summer, the scene differs considerably. The crowds are thinner, foam boards are replaced by genuine fiberglass boards and the waves become slightly more hollow, especially during the fall when the Santa Ana winds blow offshore. Surfing is best during the morning (most afternoons are blown out) on a medium tide.

BEACH KEY

Lifeguard

Surfing

Swimming

Bodyboarding

Skate Trail

Bike Trail

Dogs Allowed

Doggy Bags

Parking Fee

Huntington Cliffs

BEACH ACCESS: Located along Sea Point Avenue and the Pacific Coast Highway in Huntington Beach. Take the 405 freeway south. Exit Beach Boulevard west. Turn right onto the Pacific Coast Highway. Turn left into the metered parking lot at Sea Point Avenue. BEACH HOURS: 5:00 A.M. - 10:00 P.M.

This beach is for the dogs. Located between Golden West Street and Sea Point Avenue, Huntington Cliffs is technically part of Huntington Pier, but due to its popularity among dogs and their owners it deserves its own review.

The difference in atmosphere between these two beaches is immediately apparent. While Huntington Pier is filled with copper-toned sunbathers, scantily clad roller-bladers and competitive surf 'gromits', Huntington Cliffs, also known as Dog Beach, is filled with small, middle-sized, and large furry, four-legged animals. Together they run in groups frolicking in the crashing surf, retrieving sticks from down shore, chasing their canine friends and glorying in their newly discovered freedom.

Their owners are equally thrilled to have found an ideal place to play with their pets. It's a pleasure to witness the exchange of love between humans and animals. On weekends the

grown-ups and their dogs travel far distances to take advantage of this unique opportunity for camaraderie. Some people are happy just to parade their pets along the beach. Others, perhaps more inventive, create make-shift sleds fashioned from skate boards or roller-blades which the hounds tow along the boardwalk. And some proudly flaunt their pet's water skills and agility by tandem surfing across rolling waves all the way to shore.

It is apparent that Dog Beach brings joy to dogs and their owners. But, as often happens there are clouds appearing over this sunlit picture: The City of Huntington Beach is attempting to restrict summer hours or worse still, prohibit dogs altogether due to neglect of rules and regulations by visitors. The Preservation Society of Huntington Dog Beach has thus far been successful in keeping the beach open for dogs. They have installed doggie-bag dispensers, organized monthly beach clean-ups and employed two beach keepers to clean up anything that dog owners may have missed. Still, it is obvious that it is up to the visitors to obey the rules and keep this beach for the dogs.

SURF REPORT

Huntington Cliffs' slow rolling waves, sheltered beach strand and comparatively uncrowded waves make it a mecca for longboarders and beginning surfers. A medium tide on a west swell brings in decent rights and lefts. However, if you are looking for a more advanced ride on hollow-shaped cylinders, wait for the offshore Santa Ana winds that frequently blow in the fall.

BEACH KEY

- Lifeguard
- Surfing
- Swimming
- Bodyboarding
- Volleyball
- Bike Trail
- Skate Trail
- Snack Bar
- Restaurants
- Beach Rentals
- Shopping
- R.V. Camping
- Public Showers
- Restrooms
- Parking Fee

Huntington Pier

BEACH ACCESS: Located along the Pacific Coast Highway and Main Street in Huntington Beach. Take the 405 freeway to Beach Boulevard, exit south. After several miles Beach Boulevard dead ends at the Pacific Coast Highway. Turn right onto the Pacific Coast Highway. Turn left at Main Street into the parking lot.
BEACH HOURS: 5:00 A.M. - 10:00 P.M.

Huntington Pier is far more than a beach; it is the epicenter of the city featuring an endless array of sports competitions, dance performances, outdoor concerts plus shops and eateries all within walking distance.

Every year over nine million visitors arrive, intent on discovering for themselves the utopian 'California Dream' and where better to find it than at the world renowned Surf City, U.S.A.

In the summer, this wide beach overflows with people. From the Pier Plaza Promenade one can encompass a colorful mish-mash of renegade surfers, barely clad sun-worshipers, roller-bladers and bikers all celebrating their good fortune at living and vacationing in one of the most famous surfer's beach in America, rivaled only by Hawaii's Pipeline.

Here too is the locale where most surf and beach

competitions are held. Weekly amateur surf contests, hosted by a wide range of groups from Boy Scout troops to longboard clubs, give neophytes an opportunity to learn how to perform under pressure. The ideal time to attend is during professional surf contests such as the Gotcha Pro when hordes of Orange County citizens gather to support their heroes. The beach then becomes a mad riot of color, tents, sand, suntan oil and people. Often spectators are caught up in the competitive spirit and neighboring groups will engage in debates, ranging from friendly to hostile, over who will win and who will lose. The excitement is contagious and spreads to the shore with professional volleyball tournaments, roller hockey games, trick bike riding, skateboard ramp competitions and kite flying contests as well as a children's fishing derby.

At the north side of the Pier, surfing is taken seriously, performed on a grand scale and with fervent dedication. On any given day, Huntington's local tribe of surfers, 'mavericks' if you will, vie for the best waves. This is a unique gang, local boys flaunting tattooed bodies, dread locks, facial piercings and occasionally goatees as they zigzag across towering billows and shoot through cylindrical tubes in an almost supernatural manner. They, similar to the natives of Hawaii, do not share their break with outsiders. In fact, they often have difficulty sharing the ocean with the anglers fishing from the pier. It is not uncommon for fishermen to lose their poles to the fury of a surfer who has been hooked too many times. Therefore, it is prudent for novice surfers to ride the breaks north towards Huntington Cliffs. And after a long session they can soak up the sunshine and perhaps daydream of one day out-surfing those 'surf-rats' on the north side of the Pier.

SURF REPORT

There are almost always waves at Huntington Pier. An outer sandbar stretches offshore generating variable peaks on both sides of the wharf. They may not always be perfect barrels, but they're generally good shaped and fun.

The best time to surf is in the winter during a medium tide when the crowds are thinner and the deep ocean currents off the Aleutian Islands sweep across the Pacific ocean towards the California coast. This is when Huntington Pier, like other west facing beaches in California, 'goes off'. Thick walls of water, often as high as ten feet, come barreling toward the shore.

Surfing is blackballed June 15 - September 15 on the south side of the pier 11:00 A.M - 5:00 P.M.

BEACH KEY

Lifeguard

Swimming

Bodyboarding

Bike Trail

Skate Trail

Basketball

Volleyball

Snack Bars

Beach Rentals

Bird Watching

Fire Rings

Public Showers

Restrooms

Visitor Center

Parking Fee

Huntington State

BEACH ACCESS: From the 405 freeway, exit Beach Boulevard west. Continue several miles to the Pacific Coast Highway, turn south. Park at one of the four State Park lots: Brookhurst Street, Magnolia Street, Newland Street, or Beach Boulevard.
BEACH HOURS: 6:00 A.M. - 10:00 P.M.

Perhaps the biggest appeal of Huntington State Beach is its easy access and ample parking. Four entrances (located along the Pacific Coast Highway at Brookhurst Street, Magnolia Street, Newland Street and Beach Boulevard), 2,500 parking spaces and 2.5 miles of wide clean sands bustling with people and festivities make this beach a favorite among families from nearby inland cities.

Huntington State Beach features a whole host of recreational activities. The more popular are biking and roller-blading along the 8.5 mile beachfront trail. On summer weekends, it is customary to see throngs of people carried away in the spirit of lighthearted play. They skate and bike zealously from one end of the multi-use trail to the other, oftentimes colliding into people who block their path. Thankfully, in an effort to create a safer environment, the city has established 'Rules of the Road' and strictly enforces a 10 miles per hour speed limit on the

Beach

trail. In the water, however, a different set of rules apply: Surfing is blackballed!

The City of Huntington Beach, commonly dubbed 'Surf City, U.S.A.', is probably best known for its ever-present surfing waves. That's why many visitors are surprised to find that Huntington State Beach blackballs surf-boarders in the summer months. The glorious billowing waves are left to ecstatic bodyboarders, bodysurfers and swimmers who no longer have to worry about sharing waves with surfers or dodging their runaway surfboards. And the surf-boarders, well, they make certain to park in the Brookhurst lot and walk a few yards south to Santa Ana River Jetties where surfing is allowed year round.

Located at the southern end of the park is a California least tern natural preserve. May through August these endangered birds make Huntington State Park their nesting ground. A chicken-wire fence separates the preserve from the rest of the beach, but a pair of binoculars and the right vantage point may offer a view of one of these rare birds. In addition, interpretive signs and programs hosted by the California State Park system are an interesting way to learn more about biological diversity and ecology. Call the Huntington State Park for dates and times on Interpretive Programs. (714) 536-1454

Finally, a wonderful way to end the day is a cookout at one of the three hundred fire rings and a replay of the highlights of the day. Make certain to claim your fire ring early because in the summer they go fast.

Surf Report

Hungtington State's surf break is similar to that of Huntington Pier's but without the crowds. Variable peaks break left and right over an outer sandbar. Usually, this break is slightly smaller and less hollow than the Pier, but many prefer to sacrifice the shape then compete with crowds.

During the summer surfing is blackballed June 15 - September 15 from 10:00 A.M. - 5:00 P.M. But you can still surf by parking in the Brookhurst parking lot and walking a short distance south to Santa Ana River Jetties.

Newport Beach

If there is one coastal city in Orange County that should not be missed, it would have to be Newport Beach. Set against the backdrop of the Pacific ocean, this small but lively resort area offers visitors everything from exploring ecological preserves to sunbathing on urban beaches and enjoying carnival rides at a bayside amusement park.

A trip to Newport Beach should begin along Newport peninsula where visitors can eat, drink, and stroll all within a few feet of the beach. Restaurants specializing in fresh seafood and fruity blended drinks, plus bars and pubs, playing everything from calypso music to rock 'n roll, create a festive and energetic atmosphere almost every day and night during the summer, and on weekends during the off-season.

Further south along the peninsula is the Historic Balboa Fun Zone. Built in the early 20th century, this bayside amusement park, replete with a Ferris wheel, carousel, arcades, photo booths, gift shops and restaurants could be taken straight out of a 1920's black and white movie. Families and teens, often sporting salt stained surf trunks and bikinis, make their way from the beach and pier (located directly across the street) to the Fun Zone where parasailing, jet skiing, sport fishing and renting anything from a tandem bike to sailboats are also available. It's a hard to beat combination: A fabulous beach and pier, great waves, and good fun!

While visiting this area be sure to stop by the historic Balboa Pavilion. Built in 1905, this building was crowned as the 'birthplace of swing and dance' when big named bands such as Count Basie, and Benny Goodman would play for people who had traveled to Newport Beach on the Red Line electric cars. Today, visit its lobby to see framed photographs chronicling life in Newport Beach since 1920. This is also the location for departure for the Newport harbor cruise, whale-watching tours, water taxis to Catalina Island, Christmas boat parade and the annual sailboat race from Newport Beach to Ensenada, Mexico.

As the second largest pleasure-craft harbor in the country, Newport Beach has attracted many famous people (John Wayne, James Cagney and Shirley Temple to name a few) and has also served as the backdrop for well-known movies and television series such as Treasure Island and Giligan's Island. Sightseers can board one of many Newport harbor cruises to see the stars' homes and filming sites and learn how Newport Beach was created.

Situated across the channel from the Balboa Fun Zone is the enchanting residential community of Balboa Island. Perhaps the most charming route to the island is via the Balboa Auto Ferry located at the end of Main Street in the heart of the historic Fun Zone. For about fifty cents per person, the floating barge motors across the canal, and in about two minutes brings visitors to an island with Cape Cod styled homes and pleasure boats that lie careened along its small bay beaches. From the ferry terminal, stroll along the waterfront to Marine Avenue where there are gift shops and outdoor cafes.

One of the crowning jewels of Newport Beach is the Back Bay Ecological Preserve and Estuary. Seven hundred and fifty two acres of islands, mud flats, and creeks plus a fresh water marsh create a unique ecosystem where many different species of plants, birds and animals live. Over 35,000 birds use these wetlands as a place to rest and refuel during their winter migration. Ranger campfire programs, kayak and canoe tours, and docent-led hikes are available.

The Newport Dunes R.V. resort is one way visitors can spend more time exploring Newport Back Bay or just relax in a beautiful natural setting. Situated along the lower portion of the upper bay, vacationers can camp in R.V.s (complete with hook-ups) or tents and enjoy sunning on a sandy white beach, sailing or kayaking the bay, swimming in the pool, working on their muscles at the fitness center, dining at the Back Bay Café or watching television in the clubhouse. There is even 'room service', or to be more precise, 'R.V. service'. With all these amenities, is there any reason to stay home?

BEACH KEY

- Lifeguard
- Surfing
- Swimming
- Bodyboarding
- Skimboarding
- Fishing
- Volleyball
- Bike Trail
- Skate Trail
- Restaurants
- Snack Bars
- Beach Rentals
- Shopping
- Fire Rings
- Public Showers
- Restrooms
- Parking Fee

Newport Pier

BEACH ACCESS: Located along Newport Boulevard and 22nd Street in Newport Beach. Take the 55 freeway south. After several miles it ends. Proceed straight onto Newport Boulevard. Cross over the Pacific Coast Highway. Turn right onto 22nd Street and park in the metered lot or free along the numbered streets.
BEACH HOURS: 6:00 A.M. - 10:00 P.M.

Residents of the area around Newport Pier have been known to boast of endless summer days in a crowded yet alluring seaside community. Classic salt-box cottages border a broad beach-side trail where biking past surf shops, ice-cream parlors, and pubs is perhaps the best way to experience Newport Beach. As you ride, it is likely that you will be joined by a crowd of pedestrians, roller-bladers, and bikers who spill out from the bars into the sunlight bringing their friends with them. On summer weekends, the scene is somewhat reminiscent of David Lee Roth's *'California Girls'* music video, with scantily-clothed men and women mingling on the cobblestone street, flaunting tanned bodies and the latest in surf fashions.

On the beach, the theme varies significantly from the boardwalk.

Families maneuver their way through throngs of people, beach chairs, umbrellas, and coolers in an effort to find any space sizable enough to sit in. It's a bit of a squeeze and most adults are grateful to have found a resting place. As for the kids, the moment their feet hit the sand, they're off and running, or swimming or boarding, or joining the adults in fishing.

Speaking of fishing, there's more to Newport Pier than the boardwalk and the beach. Each morning, before the sun peeks over the horizon, skilled fishermen embark in small dory boats to net fish and lobster. When their boats are full, they motor back to the beach and starting at 11:30 a.m., they peddle their catches at an open-air market located at the base of the pier. The Dory Fishing fleet that first brought fish to Newport Beach residents in the late 1800's continues to supply the best fish in town.

SURF REPORT

Newport Pier's surf break, Blackies, a lone peak located directly in front of Blackie's Bar, typically breaks only during the winter on a mid-tide. Swells coming from the west and northwest sweep across the Pacific to form steep and peaky, fast waves that break off the sandbar.

During the summer, this break is generally small and caters to children. Surfing is blackballed from 11:00 a.m. - 5:00 p.m. And the shallow sand bar extending from the shore makes it easy for inexperienced swimmers to stand up and jump over the crumbling waves.

BEACH KEY

- Lifeguard
- Surfing
- Swimming
- Bodyboarding
- Fishing
- Volleyball
- Baseball Park
- Bike Trail
- Skate Trail
- Beach Rentals
- Amusement Park
- Restaurants
- Shopping
- Public Showers
- Fire Rings
- Restrooms
- Parking Fee

The Balboa Pier &

BEACH ACCESS: Located along Balboa Boulevard and Main Street in Newport Beach. Take the 55 freeway south. After several miles the freeway ends and becomes Newport Boulevard. Merge onto Balboa Boulevard. Turn right onto Main Street and park in the metered lot.
BEACH HOURS: 6:00 A.M. - 10:00 P.M.

Balboa Pier and Fun Zone is geared towards active families. The combination of sun and sea with a bay-side amusement park: Ferris wheel, carousel, bumper cars and a handful of 20th century 'virtual reality rides' (costing between $1.00 and $5.00) arcades, gift shops, restaurants and saloons all within a few yards of the shore make this pier many families' first choice beach destination.

For most beach connoisseurs Balboa's broad golden strand, beach-side bike/skate trail and 920 foot fishing pier is lure enough. Voted Orange County's Best Pier in the September issue of *Orange County's Best*, it is an excellent place to lunch on hamburgers and milk shakes from Ruby's, a 1950's styled diner. Or better yet, join the anglers at the end of the pier as they reel in bass, halibut, and the occasional shark. Later your catch can be barbecued at one of the many firepits located just south of the pier.

Fun Zone

Balboa Pier caters to families during the summer by blackballing surfing from 11:00 a.m. - 6:00p.m. Children can enjoy jumping the small waves or riding on the cottony froth only to be deposited onto caramel colored sands.

As far as surfing goes, this beach doesn't have much to offer. It is usually flat in the summer and even when it is breaking, 56th street, 10th street or The Wedge offers better shaped waves with bigger size.

If the action on the sea-side isn't enough for your crew, head across the street to the bustling Balboa Fun Zone and Pavilion to Davey's Locker Sportfishing for whale watching, boat charters and fishing trips. Tours of the Newport Harbor, parasailing, jet skiing, and renting anything from a tandem bike to a sail boat is also available along the boardwalk. Whether traveling by bike, boat, or foot, the famous Balboa Pavilion is a "must see". Built in the 1920's, it was known as the "birthplace of swing and dance" when visitors would travel on the Red Line electric cars to dance to the then-popular bands such as Count Basie, Benny Goodman, and Stan Kenton. That phase of the swing era may have ended, but you can still hear music on summer evenings at the beach's bandstand in Balboa Park right next to the baseball field.

BEACH KEY

Lifeguard

Surfing

Swimming

Bodyboarding

Skimboarding

Fishing

Sun Bathing

The Wedge

BEACH ACCESS: Located along East Ocean Boulevard at Jetty View Park. Take the 55 freeway south, after several miles it ends and becomes Newport Boulevard. Proceed straight on Newport Boulevard. Newport Boulevard then becomes West Balboa Boulevard. At the end of West Balboa Boulevard, turn right onto G Street and then a quick left onto Ocean Boulevard. Park free along the residential streets.
BEACH HOURS: 6:00 A.M. - 10:00 P.M.

This beach is unique. Where else would you find the majority of beachgoers dressed not in bikinis or swim trunks but in casual everyday clothes while a small number of men and even fewer women are in the ocean?

The explanation of this phenomenon lies in the name of this beach: The Wedge. When the ocean pitches swells of thirty feet and the red surf advisory flag warns swimmers of dangerous conditions, only a few daring wave riders suit up to take on the challenge. This is when surf legends are born and when 'big wave' veterans come to showcase their expertise. They navigate surfboards, bodyboards, wave-blades, kneeboards or simply their own bodies though towering and rushing tubes in order to achieve the adrenalin rush which follows a long free fall into a few inches of water. Although these aqua-men and women may choose different tools to ride The Wedge, most

have one common philosophy: 'No room for cowards' and the knowledge that once committed to a wave, any hesitation can result in serious injury from the inevitable pounding upon reaching the shore.

For the rest of us, watching from the shore is nearly as exciting and decidedly safer than entering the ocean, especially when the waves curling off the jetty, combine with the oncoming swell, and crash with so much fury that the ground vibrates. Many spectators horrified at the spectacle of such great danger, view these men and women as reckless stuntmen, but those of us who love wave-riding, and are fortunate enough to be able to watch them in action, are more likely to appreciate the passion which drives them. Despite the fact that many of these expert wave-riders wipe out on the shallow sea floor, and wake up in the emergency room of nearby Hoag Hospital with neck and back injuries, and only a few savvy individuals with superior instincts conquer The Wedge. One might ask "Is it worth the risk?" To that question, one local gave this impassioned response "It is the most important event in my life. It's where and when I find true freedom and peace. Finally, it's just me and the wave... and who wins."

18

Big wave riders might prefer surfing during a Southern Hemisphere hurricane swell when the waves can reach as high as 30 feet and maintain their shape! All types of wave-riding boards are blackballed from May 1 - October 31 between 10:00 a.m. - 5:00 p.m.

19

SURF REPORT

The Santa Ana River pushes sand into the line-up at Santa Ana River Jetties creating fast, hollow shaped waves that are best for advanced shortboarders. Unlike many other Newport beaches, surfing is allowed year round here. Afternoons are usually blown-out, so it is best to surf in the morning when the waves are still glassy.

River Jetties

BEACH ACCESS: Located along Seashore Drive and Summit Avenue in Newport Beach. Take the Pacific Coast Highway to Orange, turn west. Turn right onto Seashore and continue straight to Summit. Park free along the residential streets and walk to the beach.
BEACH HOURS: 6:00 A.M. - 10:00 P.M.

Santa Ana River Jetties is an excellent place for those who want to bicycle, naturalize, and surf all in the same day. Begin your jaunt by biking the 30 mile long Santa Ana River trail from Riverside County line to Newport Beach. As you ride, you will discover the trail is ideally suited for hours of outdoor investigation for it combines recreation with the chance for scientific exploration. The trail winds through Coastal Sage Scrub, Riparian and Oak Woodland habitats and features rest areas, parks, salt marshes and ponds. It's worth bringing your camera since you may have the opportunity to see endangered birds such as the bald eagle, California least tern, and the California brown pelican.

You will also want to make sure to bring your surfboard (preferably on a board rack) and swimsuit since the route ends at one of the best surf beaches in Newport: Santa Ana River Jetties. And what better reward, after a long ride, than cooling off in the Pacific Ocean.

As far as beaches go, this one isn't much to look at. A broad strand divided in two by a large river mouth, the southern end bordered by quaint shore homes, the northern end backed by tall, cement oil derricks, and offering little in terms of amenities. The good news, however, is that the crowds are thin, volleyball courts ample, surf hollow, and there is plenty of room for a game of tackle football.

China Cove

BEACH ACCESS: Located along Ocean Boulevard and Fernleaf Avenue in Corona del Mar. Take the Pacific Coast Highway to Marguerite Avenue, turn west. Turn right onto Ocean Boulevard. Proceed straight ½ mile to Fernleaf Avenue. Walk down a moderately sloping hill to the beach.
BEACH HOURS: 6:00 A.M. - 10:00 P.M.

Just north of the crowds and hubbub of Big Corona lies a quiet, still-water bay beach, China Cove, that beckons families to come relax on its caramel-colored shores and swim in its calm, blue waters.

Here the waves ripple rather than crash and the shallow, sandy sea floor makes it fun and safe for the kids. On warm summer days, children delight in playing king of the raft, plunging into the bay from inflatable row boats, and drifting on floats along the sun-drenched waters.

Adults can enjoy a game of volleyball, lap swimming, or simply lounging beachside while watching the boats cruise the channel.

One of the best times to visit China Cove is during the Newport Beach Christmas Boat Parade. Boats, trimmed with tinsel and colorful lights sail around Newport Harbor and turn around in front of China Cove. Families find that it is a wonderful way to embrace the Christmas spirit and ring in the coming season.

BEACH KEY

Lifeguard

Surfing

Swimming

Bodyboarding

Scuba Diving

Volleyball

Beach Rentals

Snack Bar

Fire Rings

Public Showers

Restrooms

Parking Fee

21

DIVE REPORT

Sheltered calm waters, easy beach access and a sandy ocean floor interspersed with small reefs offer divers views of sand dollars, scallops, sea fans, small lobster, garibaldi, and anemones.

For a more interesting dive, explore the reefs off Inspiration Point. The walk is more difficult, but well worth the effort.

Big Corona

BEACH ACCESS: Located along Ocean Boulevard in Corona del Mar. Take the Pacific Coast Highway to Corona del Mar. Turn west onto Marguerite. Turn right onto Ocean Boulevard. Proceed two blocks to the metered parking lot and walk to the beach.
BEACH HOURS: 6:00 A.M. - 10:00 P.M.

Equipped with a wide coastline, two snack bars, beach rentals (chairs, umbrellas and the like) as well as showers, restrooms, and manicured lawns, Big Corona has nearly all the luxuries of home. It is often extremely crowded and the ambiance is more of a "party scene" than at other beaches.

Big Corona is one beach with two separate beach accesses.

The scenic, yet more difficult access is via Inspiration Point, located at the end of Orchid Avenue where the parking is free. Its difficulty comes from the length of the steep hill to the beach. For this reason, it provides rest areas with benches and vantage points for snapshots. Once on the beach however, it is a tamer environment than the northern end.

The second beach access, which is much more easily accessible, is located off Iris Blvd. It is a short walk to the beach. You do have to pay a $6.00 fee for parking, but upon reaching the sand, you will find yourself in the very center of the action.

Little Corona

BEACH ACCESS: Located along Ocean Boulevard and Poppy in Corona del Mar. Take the Pacific Coast Highway to Corona del Mar. Turn west onto Poppy. Proceed two blocks to Ocean Boulevard. Park free along the residential streets and walk down a moderately steep hill to the beach.
BEACH HOURS: 6:00 A.M. - 10:00 P.M.

BEACH KEY

Lifeguard

Swimming

Surfing

Scuba Diving

Snorkeling

Tide Pools

Public Showers

Restrooms

22

One of Orange County's most breathtaking vistas is from the bluff-top bench overlooking Little Corona Beach. From this vantage point one can get a superior view of a solitary sea arch, tide pools, and the series of small pocket coves that line the coast. A closer view, with its own rewards can be achieved by descending a steep footpath that winds alongside million dollar homes bedecked with sprays of colorful flowers, ending at a large open cove with easily accessible tide pools.

This rocky stretch of shoreline located at the south end of the same beach, is why visitors return to Little Corona each summer. During low tide, the water recedes to unveil limpets and mussels tightly fastened to rock ledges. Also, shallow clear pools teeming with sea life should pique childrens' interest, and give them a good opportunity for hands-on-discovery.

DIVE REPORT

The best part of Little Corona is under water. Large sand patches, kelp beds, and shallow and deep reef systems harbor kelp bass, horn sharks, and rockfish. Diving is good for all skill levels.

SURF REPORT

A strong south swell is the only time Little Corona breaks. Thick barrels peel right and then close out directly over a rocky reef. There is time to pull a few maneuvers before having to bail out and wait for the next wave.

Laguna Beach

aguna is definitely one of the best known coastal towns in California. But its fame has less to do with its beaches than with its reputation as an "Artists' Colony." This dates back to1903 when the artist Norman St. Claire, having traveled from his home in San Francisco to Laguna Beach, first brought Laguna's magnificent seascapes to canvas. His work was so highly acclaimed, that his style, including that of his imitators, was thenceforth known as'California Impressionism.'

In the following years many artists including sculptors, photographers, and writers have followed in St. Claire's footsteps, and vacationers still flock to this town hoping to gain inspiration from its art festivals and scenic beauty.

The Laguna Beach Sawdust Festival (July through August) is one of the events. Here is the best time and place to buy locally-made arts and crafts. A wide variety of novelties ranging from ceramic turtle flutes and African bongo drums to Impressionist-style seascapes and hand blown glass can be purchased at a fraction of the price of galleries in town. The name, 'Sawdust', in case you're curious, comes from the chosen ground cover.

However, the most celebrated event in Laguna is the Pageant of the Masters. In July and August it provides a unique and memorable experience. These 'tableaux vivant' (living pictures) have been staged by the residents of Laguna since 1933. Located along Laguna Canyon Road in the Irvine Bowl the 2,600 seat amphitheater, nestled within a canyon setting and usually canopied by a starlit sky, provides an attractive setting for the presentation of living tableaus, closely resembling famous art; ranging from Da Vinci and the

Venus de Milo to Picasso and Norman Rockwell. The results are eerily identical to the original and many skeptics find it impossible to believe that these figures are living people. Perhaps in reply, the pageant always includes a 'builder's piece' where the first view is under authentic lighting and the human beings, their costumes and the background appears three dimensional. Abruptly, it shifts to technical lighting where the *mise en scene* then appears two dimensional. Each piece is accompanied by live music and narration in keeping with the tradition of a great performance. (Tickets range from ten to fifty dollars depending on the location of the seats. And the amphitheater is usually sold out.)

Nearly three million people visit Laguna Beach each year, and while many come for the aesthetics, others prefer the beaches and come back year after year. There are two types of beaches in Laguna and each offers something different to the active beachgoer.

Small hidden coves such as Moss, Woods and Table Rock have the romantic appeal similar to that of the French Riviera. Steep palisades, which in the spring are flecked with brilliant yellow and purple flowers, give way to fluffy white sand and crystal blue waters. Snorkeling, scuba diving, and tide pooling top the list of water sport activities here.

On the other hand, wide open strands such as Aliso and Main are less fanciful but offer some of the best on-shore sports: volleyball, basketball, hiking, and biking. Whichever you chose, Laguna's beaches are certain to enchant almost everyone.

BEACH KEY

Lifeguard

Surfing

Bodyboarding

Body Surfing

Skimboarding

Scuba Diving

Snorkeling

Spearfishing

Tide Pools

Volleyball

Rollerblading

Bike Trails

Hike Trails

Bird Watching

Tent Camping

Picnic Tables

Public Showers

Restrooms

Visitor Center

Parking Fee

Crystal Cove

BEACH ACCESS: Located along the Pacific Coast Highway between Corona del Mar and Laguna Beach. Take highway 133 west to the Pacific Coast Highway, turn right. Continue two miles north and turn into one of the four State Park entrances: El Moro, Reef Point, Los Trancos, Pelican Point.
BEACH HOURS: 6:00 A.M. - Sunset

Crystal Cove State Park is possibly the most spectacular beach in Orange County. And yet it receives only 500,000 visitors each year. Perhaps it's because Crystal Cove lies off the last undeveloped stretch of the Pacific Coast Highway, or maybe it's because the accesses are slightly more challenging than at other beaches. But whatever the reason, its shores continue to lie undiscovered and untouched.

Far more than a beach, Crystal Cove State Park is actually a canyon-ocean oasis consisting of 2,200 acres of rolling hills, 1,140 acres of ocean dedicated as an underwater marine reserve, and 3.5 miles of coastline back-dropped by steep palisades, which in the spring presents a stunning panorama of gold, purple and white wild flowers against the turquoise-blue waters of the pacific.

Five named beaches: Treasure Cove, Historic Crystal Cove, 3.5 Cove, Scotchman's Cove and Muddy Creek collectively form Crystal Cove State Park's beaches.

Treasure Cove, accessed via Pelican Point parking lots number one and two at State Park exit, feels like coastal California some 200 years ago. An intimate enclave where sapphire-blue water rolls onto a tawny-colored shoreline and craggy cliffs shine copper-colored in the sunlight; visitors will discover a beach that warrants exploration. At low tide, stratified rock benches that have been chiseled away from centuries of wind and waves look like geological antiques. And with close investigation, one will discover that inside their cracks, crevices and holes lies a macroscopic aquatic world teeming with hermit crabs, limpets, chitons, anemones and urchins.

Further south, Historic Crystal Cove, reached via Los Tranocs exit is a small seaside hamlet where cottages built from beached driftwood, surfboards, palm fronds and ship wrecks, are nestled into the cliff and onto the shores. A visit to this cove brings beachgoers back to the depression days of the early 1930's, when life for many throughout America was grim. But for the small group of people living here at what is now Crystal Cove State Park 'grim' was not acceptable. Hopeful for a happier life, they united together to build this unique community. Today, escape to this seaside haven and experience for yourself Crystal Cove life, where responsibility and concern are left to the modern world and only surfing, diving, volleyball, and beach luaus remain.

3.5 Cove's blufftop trail, accessed via the Reef Point exit at the northern parking lots, is so beautiful that often visitors become enamored with this beach before even reaching its shores. The ¾ mile flowery path, which in the spring is a riot of yellow and gold wild flowers, appeals to almost all your senses. Offshore breezes carry floral scents on warm air currents, and the constant hum of cicadas, perhaps in response to the squeaks and chirps from squirrels and birds, resonates like a vibrating string from an electric guitar. The beach itself is a long and lovely crescent, framed by tide pools on either end: Rocky Bite to the north and Pelican Point to the south. Both tide pools are spectacular, but Pelican Point offers more adventure. Split Rock, a rock island measuring roughly 35 feet long and 15 feet wide, lies directly offshore of Pelican Point. At low tide, don mask and fins and amble across the small hopscotch of pools and boulders to the island where you can explore underwater caves and caverns.

The blufftop vantage point overlooking Scotchman's Cove, located behind restroom number five at Reef Point exit, affords visitors a stunning kaleidoscope of color. Light and dark blues, deep greens and brilliant golds compel them to make their way down the uneven wooden stairway leading to the beach. Once onshore, beachgoers find a beach suitable for a variety of water sports: surfing, snorkeling, scuba diving and swimming.

Muddy Creek, reached via a short, steep footpath, which is located behind restroom number six at Reef Point exit, is where families come to build memories. Bring your ice-chest and sunscreen and join the mosaic of families picnicking underneath beach umbrellas and scuttling across the white wash on bodyboards and floats. Perhaps the most child friendly beach at Crystal Cove State Park (the only cove with a sandy sea floor), families find that, in terms of enjoyment, the sky is the limit- or in this case-the beach.

DIVE REPORT

Crystal Cove's 1,140 acre underwater park, excellent visibility (as deep as 30 feet in winter) and underwater reef systems make it an ideal place to scuba dive and snorkel.

Reef Point, Rocky Bight, Pelican Point and Treasure Point all feature excellent diving however, Scotchman's Cove's Reef Point is the best. Follow the reef from the beach to Split Rock, the rock island located offshore, to explore underwater channels and caves. Be aware of strong currents when exploring this area.

SURF REPORT

Crystal Cove State Beach may not have fast waves such as Trestles or tubing peaks such as Salt Creek, but it does offer fewer crowds, which means less competition for waves.

The surf breaks and their best swell directions are as follows: Treasure Point, Reef Point, Abalone Point (south & southwest) Pelican Point, Boneyard and Rivermouth (north & northwest) All break best on a rising mid-tide.

INTERPRETIVE PROGRAMS

Crystal Cove State Park features complimentary docent-led hikes of their back country and beaches. Visitors can choose from a variety of recreational and educational tours where docents teach about the flora, fauna and natural history of the area. Back country tours include, guided hikes (3-5 miles), guided full-moon mountain bike rides, bat walks winter solstice hikes, and astronomy night.

Beach tours include tide pool walks, sunset-moonlight beach walks, Earth Day tree planting and habitat restoration, and gray whale programs.

Crystal Cove's Interpretive program schedule varies. It is best to call their interpretive program hotline for exact dates and times.

Phone: (949) 497-7648

El Moro

PARK ACCESS: Located along the Pacific Coast Highway and El Moro between Laguna Beach and Corona del Mar. Take the Pacific Coast Highway to El Moro, turn east. Proceed straight and park in the State Park's lot.

PARK HOURS: 6:00 A.M. - Sunset

The San Joaquin hills, Crystal Cove State Park's back county, features 22 miles of nature trails that traverse grassland peaks, riparian woodlands, coastal sage scrub habitats, and sycamore oak woodland canopies. Many visitors come here to hike, mountain bike and horseback ride down to the valley floor and up to the canyon ridges all the while watching Cooper's hawks and white-tailed kites circle for prey; deer drinking from streams, and lizards sunning themselves on rocks.

In addition, many areas in the backcounty give visitors insight into the natural history and life of the Juaneno Indians who once lived here. One such place is Indian Rock located just beyond a sycamore oak woodland. Deep indentations in the rock are a sign that the rock was used by Native Americans to grind acorns into meal.

If one finds the day is too short, consider staying overnight at one of Crystal Cove's three environmental campgrounds: Upper Moro, Lower Moro or Deer Canyon. It's a bit of hike (3 miles each way), but it is definitely worth the effort!

Crescent Bay

BEACH ACCESS: Located along Cliff Drive in North Laguna Beach. Take the Pacific Coast Highway to Cliff Drive, turn west. Park free along the residential streets and follow a moderately steep stairway to the beach.

BEACH HOURS: 6:00 AM - 10:00 P.M.

This three hundred foot cove situated at the northern end of Laguna Beach explodes with colorful beach umbrellas, which on weekends are packed so tightly that often the rim of one touches the next. Join the crowds in sand castle building, wave riding, diving or simply relaxing with a pleasant walk along the shore.

Some beachgoers may prefer a less crowded weekday, when all the pursuits listed above are also possible.

For the adventurous, on the south end you can find Barnacle Ledge, a long natural jetty, which as the name implies, is covered with barnacles and mussels. With careful observation one can find hermit crabs and other tidal life

among these rocks. During low tide, the more ambitious can journey across the northernmost cliffs to a secret cove. The next step requires effort and some caution. The only way to get on shore is to find the rope and use it to repel down a small ledge into the water, then swim to the beach. On occasion, seals from nearby Seal Rock bask on these shell strewn shores.

28

DIVE REPORT

Crescent's diving is similar to other destinations in Laguna Beach - large sand patches, rocky reefs, and steep walls. But this beach has one added attraction - Seal Rock and the handful of sea lions that make this their home. Here divers can swim alongside ocean mammals while taking in the sights of the Pacific.

BEACH KEY

- Lifeguard
- Swimming
- Bodyboarding
- Skimboarding
- Scuba Diving
- Snorkeling
- Spear Fishing
- Tide Pools

DIVE REPORT

At Shaw's Cove, divers can explore underwater caves and rock ledges. Located north, just before the point, a large underwater cave leads to many smaller ones where octapi, moray eels, and a variety of fish can be seen. Surges and strong currents are common in the cave so only experienced divers should explore this area.

Shaw's Cove

BEACH ACCESS: Located along Cliff Drive in North Laguna Beach. Take the Pacific Coast Highway to Fairview, turn west. Turn left onto Cliff Drive. Park between Fairview and Wave Street at the meters or free along the residential streets. Walk down a moderately difficult stairway to the beach.

BEACH HOURS: 6:00 A.M. - 10:00 P.M.

Shaw's Cove is beautiful. It has a small waterfront strand that is back-dropped by lofty sandstone cliffs and etched with spectacular tide pools. Brilliantly clear waters and flourishing sea life make Shaw's Cove a favorite among divers. In fact, because the dive conditions are so ideal, many scuba schools bring their classes here. For this reason, Shaw's gets very crowded during the summer months. But not to worry, dive classes have to be out of the water by 10:00 a.m.

Fisherman's Cove

BEACH ACCESS: Located along Cliff Drive in Laguna Beach. Take the Pacific Coast Highway to Cliff Drive, turn west and follow Cliff Drive to the left around the bend. Park at the meters or free along the residential Streets. Follow a short stairway and alley to the beach.
BEACH HOURS: 6:00 A.M. - 10:00 P.M.

30

Fisherman's Cove, easily reached through a short stairway and a narrow alley, is actually a sliver of sandy beach too tiny for most typical onshore activities. However, for those who delight in deep ocean sports, this is an ideal location. Here, when the sea is calm, the waves softly caress the shore, making an esay entrance and exit for scuba divers drawn to this place by expansive reef

systems located directly off shore, and by the vibrantly colored fish darting between rocks or retreating in canyons.

The most exciting times at this beach occur when storms are brewing in the South and Southwest regions. These create dynamic conditions at Fisherman's Cove. Fast rolling side waves crash over the reefs

with so much force that often the ground shakes. It is fascinating to observe, but the real excitement occurs when a few daring bodyboarders are confident enough (or rash enough) to dare maneuver their board barreling through an obstacle course of boulders and reefs. The boarders choose this moment in nature's fury to risk all in hopes of achieving the ultimate thrill.

BEACH KEY

- Lifeguard
- Swimming
- Scuba Diving
- Snorkeling
- Kayaking
- Tide Pools
- Spear Fishing
- Parking Fee
- Dogs Allowed (Restricted Hours)

DIVE REPORT

Fisherman's Cove is more like a lagoon than the Pacific Ocean. Protected by reef formations on either end, this beach usually has small or no waves.

Seventy yards offshore, a reef breaks the surface of the water: Splash Rock. This is one of Laguna's most interesting reefs. Deep canyons, crevices and steep walls plus a family of rays, eels, and reef fish abound here.

BEACH KEY

Lifeguard

Surfing

Bodyboarding

Swimming

Scuba Diving

Snorkeling

Skate Trail

Lawn Bowling

Tide Pools

Park

Barbecues

Public Showers

Restrooms

Parking Fee

Dogs Allowed
(Restricted Hours)

Heisler Park

BEACH ACCESS: Located along Cliff Drive in Laguna Beach. Take the Pacific Coast Highway to Cliff Drive, turn west. Park along the meters or free along the residential streets. Take one of four marked pathways to the coves below.
BEACH HOURS:6:00 A.M. - 10:00 P.M.

These beaches contains so many lovely vistas and pleasurable activities that it is almost impossible to manage it all in one day.

However, a good place to begin is on the bluff top, Heisler Park, which overlooks the northern coast of Laguna Beach. Here visitors can experience all the sights and sounds of the beach without ever getting their feet sandy. Nevertheless, they can still explore cactus gardens, skate or walk along the pathway, compete in lawn bowling and shuffle-board, or if desired, relax on one of the benches offering a 180 degree view of the coastline and the coves directly below. Still, for many visitors the favorite pastime is cooking out at one of the many picnic sites scrupulously hidden in enclaves throughout the grounds. Four short stairways lead down to a series of small pocket coves: Rockpile, Monument Point, Picnic, and Diver's Cove.

Fortunately, these coves can be discovered easily, for their names were inspired by their seascape.

Rockpile Beach has a well deserved reputation for some of the best preserved tide pools. At low tide the ocean rolls back giving explorers a peek at what lives beneath the water's surface: A shallow reef carpeted with red and purple sea grass extends a hundred or so yards offshore. To the south lies the sheltered tide pools where, with little effort, you can find grazing animals: Hermit crabs, sea slugs, sea urchins, and sea anemones. To the north lies both exposed and sheltered tide pools where you may find filter feeders such as mussels, limpets, and barnacles. During high tide, water covers the entire strand, virtually cutting off all access. This is the ideal time to relax on one of the afore-mentioned bluff top benches and watch the small cave at the southern end of the beach where a blowhole howls as it sprays water about twenty feet into the air.

Monument Point offers one of the best exposed tide pool areas in Laguna Beach. The shore is a beach with no sand; instead, it is a rocky intertidal zone. Visitors can delight in observing shoreline crabs, mussels, and a variety of limpets (owl, keyhole, finger.) Most people visiting Monument Point are often in awe of the great rock protruding from the ocean. To get a superior view of Laguna's coastline, climb the huge rock but only at low tide. High tide will make entry and exit difficult at best and often dangerous! It is wise to follow the tide tables when exploring this particular cove at Heisler Park.

Picnic Beach is a small crescent shaped cove ringed by bluffs and small rock ledges. The shore is narrow, and on hot summer days the beach is so crowded that in order to reach the shoreline, visitors must make their way through a veritable obstacle course of scattered towels, pails, shovels, children, and beach umbrellas. The solution is to arrive early before the crowds appear and spend your day snorkeling or diving in the clear water or picnicking at the bluff top park.

Diver's Cove is known as one of the best underwater marine parks in Orange County. Magnificently diverse underwater terrain and an abundance of aquatic life make diving and snorkeling the ideal sport activities here. Similar to Picnic Beach, Diver's Cove is small and often crowded in the summer. For onshore activities such as sunbathing, smashball, or volleyball, it is best to drive south to Main Beach.

32

DIVE REPORT

Set aside as a marine life reserve, where hunting or collecting of sea life is strictly prohibited (violations are $1,000 per animal), Hiesler Park gives divers the opportunity to see various species in their natural habitat. Extensive reefs, small caves, and kelp beds are found throughout Hiesler's five coves where horn sharks, garibaldi, yellowtail, senoritas, rock wrasse and sheepshead, can be easily discovered. For more serious divers, arrive after 10:00 a.m. to avoid the crowds.

SURF REPORT

Rockpile is the only surf break at Hiesler Park. It is one of those breaks that's excellent if you make it but terrible if you don't. The take-off is directly behind a huge boulder. As you drop in, you have to get around and in front of this rock and navigate through a slalom course composed of two more large boulders. This is a fun-peeling right if you make the maze, but it can end up in disaster if you don't; the bottom is a cheese-grater of rocks and pointy things.

33

BEACH KEY

- Lifeguard
- Skimboarding
- Volleyball
- Basketball
- Chess Tables
- Shopping
- Restaurants
- Public Showers
- Restrooms
- Parking Fee

SURF REPORT

Laguna Main's shallow sandbar directly offshore creates shore breaking waves. Bodyboarders and bodysurfers must dig right or left to avoid 'going over the falls' and being pounded onto the sand.

Main Beach

BEACH ACCESS: Located along the Pacific Coast Highway and Broadway in Laguna Beach. Take the Pacific Coast Highway to Broadway and park at the meters along the highway.
BEACH HOURS: 6:00 A.M. - 10:00 P.M.

Main Beach unites the worlds of the hippie and the yuppie. Because Laguna Beach is festive and beautiful, it attracts a lively and colorful crowd which reflects its diverse culture.

On weekends, local artists set up shop along the boardwalk to display their recent 'masterpieces'. Animated street musicians, who sit cross-legged strumming their guitars and singing their latest hits add to the artistic ambiance.

On the beach's northern end, competitive volleyball and basketball games draw the best athletes while boisterous onlookers cheer for the best volleyball dives or basketball rebounds. At night this beach quiets to a low roar and offers couples a romantic stroll along the boardwalk.

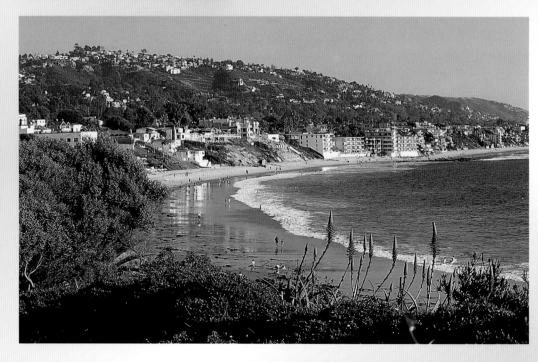

Street Beaches

BEACH ACCESS: Take the Pacific Coast Highway to Laguna Beach. Park at the meters along Pacific Coast Highway or one of the following streets: Sleepy Hollow Lane, Cleo Street, Saint Anns Drive, Thalia Street, Anita Street, Oak Street, Brooks Street, Cress Street.

BEACH HOURS: 6:00 A.M. - 10:00 P.M.

The view from the stairway is beautiful; clear blue waters with tubing waves and Catalina Island sitting on the distant horizon. Sunset walks as well as skimboarding, bodyboarding, surfing, and diving top the list of favorite beach activities.

Eight beaches: Anita, Oak, Thalia, Saint Ann's, Cleo, Brooks, Cress and Sleepy Hollow Lane are collectively known as Laguna's Street Beaches. In all, they consist of three miles of narrow white sands back-dropped by quaint beach cottages, grand resorts, galleries and small but convenient hole-in-the-wall eateries within easy walking distance.

BEACH KEY

- Lifeguard
- Surfing
- Swimming
- Bodyboarding
- Skimboarding
- Scuba Diving
- Parking Fee
- Dogs Allowed (Restricted Hours)

DIVE REPORT

Cleo Street Beach features the 130 foot *1958 Foss* barge. Located directly offshore, scuba divers can enter from the beach and explore this interesting wreck.

SURF REPORT

Surf breaks: Brooks, St. Ann's, and Thalia are all consistent peaks, but Brooks is by far the best. Three small reefs form this high quality wave. A south swell with a medium to high tide gives surfers a ride on thick, hollow bowls.

BEACH KEY

- Lifeguard
- Surfing
- Swimming
- Bodyboarding
- Spear Fishing
- Snorkeling
- Skimboarding
- Tide Pools
- Dogs Allowed (Restricted Hours)

SKIM REPORT

A soft, sandy beach and shallow sea floor make skimboarding the favored water sport at Pearl Street. For neophytes, skimboarding during low tide is best because the waves break further off-shore. The more experienced skimboarders ride during a higher tide, when the waves break near shore and offer more face for tricks.

Pearl Street

BEACH ACCESS: Located along the Pacific Coast Highway and Pearl Street in Laguna Beach. Take the Pacific Coast Highway to Pearl Street, turn west. Turn left onto Ocean Way. Park free along the residential streets then walk back to Pearl Street. The access is almost hidden behind a reflective rail at the end of the road. Walk behind the rail and proceed down a short stairway to the beach.
BEACH ACCESS: 6:00 A.M . - 10:00 P.M.

Discover the simple life at Pearl Street Beach. The picture says it all. This quaint Laguna Beach cove has white, sandy shores with occasional strong, shore breaking waves that are great for skimboarding.

Along the south end is a natural sea arch. Pass through the arch at low tide to find two blowholes, tide pools and abundant sea life.

Wood's Cove

BEACH ACCESS: Located along the Pacific Coast Highway and Diamond in Laguna Beach. Take the Pacific Coast Highway to Diamond, turn west. Turn right onto Ocean Way. Park free along the residential streets. Walk down a moderately steep stairway to the beach.

BEACH HOURS: 6:00 A.M. - 10:00 P.M.

36

A large jutting rock divides this Laguna beach into two small coves. Each cove is set between high cliffs and each offers different activities to the beachgoer.

The southern cove is noted for its serenity and its thundering shore-breaking waves. Mussel shells scattered along the shoreline attest to abundant sea life. Snorkel or scuba dive in either cove to discover a tranquil world of marine life living below the foaming white turmoil.

The northern cove not only offers excellent diving beyond the wave break, but is good for bodysurfing and tide pool exploration.

During low tide, hike across the rocks to see these rocky intertidal pools plus two small blowholes and a sea arch.

Or if you'd rather, simply relax onshore and watch as locals play frisbee and smashball, and as divers emerge with nets full of fish.

To see a variety of sea life and ocean terrain head to Wood's Cove. The southern inlet has a sandy bottom and a small kelp forest that lays just offshore. The northern inlet has a large rock bench and overhangs where sea critters reside.

37

BEACH KEY

- Lifeguard
- Swimming
- Scuba Diving
- Snorkeling
- Fishing
- Tide Pools
- Dogs Allowed (Restricted Hours)

DIVE REPORT

Moss, one of Laguna's prettiest dive sites, features clear waters and abundant marine life. On the south side, roughly 50 yards offshore, is an underwater ridge that ascends about twenty feet from the sea floor. This is a good place to find lobster, gorgorians, and sea anemeones as well as game fish such as halibut and kelp bass.

WARNING!

Moss occasionally has strong surges and rip currents. Check diving conditions with the *Laguna Beach Surf Report* before exploring this cove.

Moss Cove

BEACH ACCESS: Located along the Pacific Coast Highway and Moss Street in Laguna Beach. Take the Pacific Coast Highway to Moss Street, turn west. Park free along the residential streets. Follow a moderately difficult stairway to the beach.
BEACH HOURS: 6:00 A.M. - 10:00 P.M.

Moss is a secluded, sun-drenched beach checkered by sand and rocky reefs. It is the smallest cove in Laguna so it is often difficult to find a place to sit.

During high tide, water covers the majority of the beach strand and forces visitors high atop rocks and ledges to avoid getting wet. This, however, is the best time to listen as elaborate rock formations act as a natural amphitheater and echo the sounds of the crashing waves. During low tide, a small rocky intertidal area is exposed, including a bench that's dotted with intertidal life such as small acorn barnacles, chitons, and a variety of limpets. In the pools and crevices, sea anemones, sea stars, and crabs abound.

Swimming in these cool, clear waters may look inviting but it can often be very difficult. The cove is surrounded by shallow finger reefs that extend from the shoreline to the ocean. There is really only one spot where a visitor can take a quick dip without kicking the submerged rocks directly in front of the lifeguard tower.

Victoria

BEACH ACCESS: Located along Victoria in Laguna Beach. Take the Pacific Coast Highway to Nyes Street, turn east. Turn left onto Victoria. Park free along the residential streets. Walk down a moderately difficult stairway to the beach.

BEACH HOURS: 6:00 A.M. - 10:00 P.M.

38

Victoria Beach dazzles locals and tourists with its vintage charm. This classic broad shore beach boasts of tide pools, clear waters, and a replica of a 1920's fairytale castle and high-tide swimming pool. Often, artists and photographers set up easels and tripods in an effort to capture its beauty on canvas and film.

Bursting with sea life, Victoria's tide pools are some of the best in Laguna Beach. Shoreline crabs scurry about the rocks, urchins strategically hide under ledges, and limpets securely fasten themselves to large boulders. Adding to all the action is a large blowhole that thunders and sprays water into the sky.

In the center of the tide pool area is a large structure that looks like a princess castle. The castle is really an elaborate staircase leading from a bluff-top house to the tide pools and a man made high-tide swimming pool coined "the old woman's bathtub". It is so named because in the 1920's many bathing beauties would come here to swim. Today, bring your toddlers and let them chase the small fish around the pool or just take a dip to cool off.

SKIM REPORT

A powerful shorebreak, sandy sea floor, little competition for waves and an occasional sidewash (located on the southern end of the beach) makes Victoria one of the best skimboarding locales in Orange County. Although all tides are good, high tide offers more face for performing tricks.

BEACH KEY

Lifeguard

Swimming

Scuba Diving

Bodyboarding

Spear Fishing

Fishing

Skimboarding

Tide Pools

Sun Bathing

Park

Public Showers

Dogs Allowed (Restricted Hours)

Parking Fee

DIVE REPORT

Treasure Island offers easy and enjoyable scuba diving and snorkeling. Divers can explore finger and patch reefs which shelter lobster, bass, garibaldi, sea snails, sea stars, and red and purple sea urchins.

Treasure Island

BEACH ACCESS: Located along the Pacific Coast Highway and Wesley Drive in Laguna Beach. Take the Pacific Coast Highway to Wesley Drive, turn west. Park in the underground garage and walk along the bluff-top park to one of three marked pathways down to the beach.
BEACH HOURS: 6:00 A.M. - 10:00 P.M.

Treasure Island's gently rolling waves, verdant green cliffs and sandy strand have long enticed writers, photographers and artists to her shores.

For years, this beach was enjoyed almost exclusively by residents of Treasure Island Mobile Home Park because public beach access was so difficult. Today, that has all changed thanks in large part to the Montage Resort and the City of Laguna Beach. Now, visitors can park in an underground garage and stroll along a glorious seven-arce bluff-top park, replete with flowerbeds, gazebos, teak benches and artists at their easels, to one of three beach access.

The first access leads to a sandy beach strand. The waves break directly onshore making this section of beach ideal for skim-boarding. Just north is a set of wooden stairs, which leads down to a small sandy cove now re-named Goff Island Cove. The third access leads to the far end of Goff Island Cove and features a blowhole and a large tidepool area alive with shoreline crabs, urchins and anemones.

Despite Treasure Island's new resident, The Montage Resort, the beach is surprising ever as remote and serene as it has always been.

Aliso Beach

BEACH ACCESS: Located along the Pacific Coast Highway in Laguna Beach. Take the Pacific Coast Highway and turn west into Aliso Creek County Beach. Park in the metered lot and walk to the beach.

BEACH HOURS: 6:00 A.M. - 10:00 P.M.

BEACH KEY

- Lifeguard
- Swimming
- Bodyboarding
- Skimboarding
- Snack Bar
- Beach Rentals
- Fire Rings
- Public Showers
- Restrooms
- Parking Fee

40

SKIM REPORT

Home to the 'Annual Unofficial Skimboarding Contest', Aliso is one of the best known skimboarding and bodyboarding locales in Southern California. On a south swell and a low tide, Aliso's fast shore breaking barrels and occasionally thick side-wash waves are perfect for skimboarding and bodyboarding.

Situated along the Pacific Coast Highway, this is the only beach in Laguna that offers easy parking, direct beach access, beach rentals, a playground, and a snack bar. In terms of convenience, this beach is a winner.

Unfortunately, it has two severe limitations. The waves are dangerous, often breaking strongly and inconsistently. Only foolhardy beginners or those we now call "extreme" or experienced bodyboarders and skimboarders dare to ride on these challenging waves. As a matter of record, a number of serious back and neck injuries occur here each year. Water quality is the second limitation. Due to urban runoff from Aliso Creek, the ocean water and parts of the shoreline are not as clean as most people prefer. For that reason, official signs are posted warning beachgoers not to swim or bathe in the creek. To avoid or partially avoid the pollutants, swim at least 100 feet from its drainage.

Considering these warnings, the reader may wonder why many people still swim here. One local gave this curious explanation: "I'd forfeit my health for a ride on a good wave any day."

BEACH KEY

- Swimming
- Snorkeling
- Scuba Diving
- Fishing
- Spear Fishing
- Tide Pools
- Restaurants
- Sun Bathing
- Dogs Allowed (Restricted Hours)

DIVE REPORT

Table Rock's underwater terrain is primarily a sandy sea floor interspersed with a few finger reefs and rocky outcroppings. These clear waters harbor leopard sharks, rays, corbina and halibut and cater to the leisure diver verses the more serious diver and spear fisher.

Table Rock

BEACH ACCESS: Located along Table Rock and the Pacific Coast Highway in South Laguna Beach. Take the Pacific Coast Highway to Table Rock. Park free along the highway. Walk west on Table Rock, through the archway and down a long, moderately-steep stairway to the beach.
BEACH HOURS: 7:00 A.M. - 10:00 P.M.

Table Rock, probably the best kept secret of all the beaches in Laguna, is well worth the effort of discovery.

Set between high sandstone cliffs and adjacent to a thirty-two foot table rock, this beach's first pocket cove is stunning at high tide when heavy waves cast spray over the table rock. It is even more dramatic during a full moon when the high tide creates a wall of water, often reaching as high as forty feet.

But when the sea is calm, this cove is welcoming to swimmers and fishermen. Swimming in the clear green water is easy and fishing from the table rock is ideal. The center tide pool ledge provides shallow pools, convenient for preserving the day's catch.

South of this secluded cove lies yet another hidden and secluded cove which can be reached by swimming past the ledge and heading south around the bend.

(Watch for powerful waves which could push you into the cliff) This one is set between a giant cliff on the north and a natural arched cave on the south. From here, a strong swimmer has a panoramic view of the cave and also a path to a third cove which is accessed by side-stepping through the cave and then jumping from a low lying rock onto the shore.

Thousand Steps

BEACH ACCESS: Located along the Pacific Coast Highway and 10th Street in South Laguna Beach. Take the Pacific Coast Highway to 10th Street. Park free along the highway. Cross the highway and proceed down a long and very steep stairway to the beach.
BEACH HOURS: 6:00 A.M. - 9:00 P.M.

You may step to the edge of this difficult beach access and find yourself asking, "Why would I come to a beach named Thousand Steps?" But as you look out past the stairs towards the horizon, you will begin to understand why. Seemingly untouched by civilization, this beach is equally as impressive as any of Hawaii's hidden beaches. It offers pristine sandy shores, crystal clear waters, and unsurpassed skimboarding and bodyboarding waves. In fact, Thousand Steps is so renowned for its waves that professionals and amateurs alike come from all over the world to ride them.

BEACH KEY

- Lifeguard
- Swimming
- Bodyboarding
- Skimboarding
- Snorkeling
- Volleyball
- Fishing
- Tide Pools
- Public Showers
- Restrooms

SKIM REPORT

Thousand Steps is one of the best skimboarding beaches in Southern California. Many professionals and semi-professionals skim here making it a great place to watch and learn from some of the best. The beach's waves are consistent shore breaks with fast-rolling side washes that give skimboarders a long ride. Skimming is best during the summer months at high tide.

Dana Point

In the nineteenth century, Richard Henry Dana in his book of experiences as a sailor, *Two Years Before The Mast* (which changed conditions of sailors throughout the English speaking world), describes a stop at a natural cove which was, at the time, the only large port between Santa Barbara and San Diego. The handful of inhabitants of this village saw Dana as a historical hero and decided to name their city, Dana Point, after the famous author.

The sea, harbor, and beach are today almost as lovely as they were two hundred years ago, but the city itself has grown in size and population. The harbor is now a well-populated marina and is the location of the annual festivals recalling the history of the city. Each spring a Whale Festival, honors the migrating California gray whale. Ranger Campfire programs and whale watching tours teach visitors about the whale's migration patterns, mating habits, and its struggle for existence as a predator and a victim. A portion of the proceeds is donated by the city for the protection of the whales. In the fall, the city celebrates with its annual Tall Ships Festival and Great Schooner Parade. Complete with cannon battles, pirate mock trials, and shot-gun weddings, visitors will experience tales of buried treasures and thieving pirates. It's good fun!

The annual Jazz Festival, held in early summer, and the annual music festival, "Doheny Days" held in late summer, are two ways during which the city recreates the classic 1960's beach party. Bring your beach chairs, beach blankets, and sunscreen, and get ready for a wildly exciting time. The hum of the crashing waves may beckon you to grab your surfboard and head for the water, but with two

stages, food booths, fresh-made margaritas and kegs of beer, the temptation will almost certainly pass.

Year round, the harbor is one of the best recreational attractions with oceanfront boardwalks to bike, skate, and jog; calm waters to sail, kayak and jet ski; fish to catch and tide pools to investigate. Additional features include restaurants, gift shops, boat and jet ski rentals, boat launch, guest slips, fuel stations, sport fishing, and champagne cruises.

Further attractions include the Ocean Institute located on Dana Point Harbor Drive. Educational programs on marine science and maritime history as well as docent led tours of Dana's Pilgrim and the Dana Point tide pools are available.

While Dana Point attracts residents and tourists with historical celebrations and nautical sports, the true allure of the city is its beaches. At the southern end, both the beach and the sea floor are rocky. The waves are good for longboarding, and beach amenities are excellent. A long beachfront bike/skate path stretches from Capistrano Beach to Doheny State Beach. Easy accesses, snack bars, beach rentals, and grassy picnic areas with barbecues and tables make these beaches a great choice for group activities. At the northern end, both the sea floor and the beach are mostly sandy. The waves are good for longboarding and shortboarding as well as skim-boarding and bodyboarding. Clear waters and large shores make these beaches more beautiful than the southern end. Access entails walking down a rather long, steep hill and some stairs. Most Dana Point residents regard these beaches as their true home and the bluff-top civilization as, well, just a place to sleep.

BEACH KEY

- Lifeguard
- Surfing
- Swimming
- Bodyboarding
- Skimboarding
- Basketball
- Bike Trail
- Park
- Barbecues
- Snack Bar
- Beach Rentals
- Public Showers
- Restrooms
- Parking Fee

Salt Creek

BEACH ACCESS: Located along Ritz Carlton Drive in Dana Point. Take the Pacific Coast Highway to Ritz Carlton Drive, turn west. Park in the metered lot and walk down a moderately steep hill to the beach.
BEACH HOURS: 6:00 A.M. - 12 Midnight

On a bluff high above Salt Creek's wide clean sands, the great picture windows of the Ritz-Carlton Hotel add their sparkle to the sunlight as does the large green park directly to the left of the hotel.

Halfway down the bluff from the hotel is a snack bar with a fine view, where visitors can treat themselves to anything from a corn dog to a fileted fish sandwich. This area reflects South County's wealth and fashionable life style and is, therefore, one of the most glamorous locales in Orange County. The only ingredient that seems to be missing is a cocktail waitress serving margaritas to sunbathers on the shore.

Those who prefer more adventure will discover a host of possible activities: Surfing, bodyboarding, bodysurfing, skimboarding, tide pooling, sunbathing, picnicking, kite flying, and basketball.

As a matter of record, before the Ritz Carlton was built, this beach wasn't so civilized.

During the 1970's a couple of men known as the Young Brothers, erected a shack at the entrance to the beach. As cars drove down the long dirt path, the brothers held out a broom-handle, coin purse attached, to blockade the access until the visitors deposited fifty cents. Those visitors who dodged the fee were hunted down, and when found were pelted with rock salt until they paid up.

The fifty cent fee that the Young brothers charged back in the 70's almost seems like a bargain compared to today's parking prices of fifty cents every half hour.

SURF REPORT

Salt Creek has three surf breaks: The Point, Middles and Gravels. The Point, located at the southern end of the beach, is a long left that works best on a South swell. During low tide, the waves peel fast. At high tide, the break is considerably slower. In the summer the waves become a little mushy, but they still have lots of face for a fun ride.

Middles is a good bet anytime of the year. Fast and hollow waves break both right and left over a shallow sand bar. They gain more power and strength when storms brew anywhere in the Pacific. June 15-September 15, the blackball flag claims this territory for bodyboarding and swimming.

Gravels is a temperamental shore break. Seasons can go by when the waves are simply unridable. But, when the sand shifts to gravel, hollow, peaky waves form. The outside waves are best on a low tide. The inside waves are better on a medium to high tide.

BEACH KEY

- Snorkeling
- Swimming
- Tide Pools
- Spear Fishing
- Sun Bathing
- Pay Station

DIVE REPORT

A large reef extending from the beach to roughly 300 yards offshore provides excellent conditions for snorkeling. The cove is sheltered from wind and large waves therefore visibility is usually good.

Occasionally, seals make their way into the cove and can be seen snacking on red and purple urchins found on the submerged rocks. Garabali, lobster and octopi are just a few of the species that reside here.

Shell Beach

BEACH ACCESS: Located along the Pacific Coast Highway in Laguna Niguel. Take the Pacific Coast Highway to Ritz Carlton Drive, turn west. Park in the Salt Creek parking lot and walk down the hill to Salt Creek Beach. Proceed north to Monarch Bay. Hike over shoreline rocks and large boulders ¼ mile to Shell Beach. Accessible during low tide only!

BEACH HOURS: 6:00 A.M. - 12 MIDNIGHT

Shell Beach is one of the most scenic coves in Orange County. Secluded and romantic, this beach gives visitors a feeling of being marooned on a deserted island. Lofty cliffs, carpeted in lush green foliage, shelter the beach from wind. Sea surges and ebbs provide a dramatic change of scenery daily. Exploring the tide pools, snorkeling, and beach combing are just a few recommendations to while away the day at Shell Beach.

Wading and snorkeling provides swimmers with sights of green sea grass and golden-hued Garibaldi, while a hike over the northern bluffs affords a panorama stretching from Dana Point to Newport Beach. Although it is a bit of a walk to get here, it is well worth the effort!

Dana Strands

BEACH ACCESS: Located along the Pacific Coast Highway and Selva Road. Take the Pacific Coast Highway to Selva Road, turn west. Turn right into the parking lot and walk down a long stairway and steep hill to the beach.
BEACH HOURS: 6:00 A.M. - 12 Midnight

BEACH KEY

- Lifeguard
- Surfing
- Swimming
- Bodyboarding
- Skimboarding
- Tide Pools
- Public Showers
- Restrooms

48

Far from the roar of city traffic and the sometimes tedious habits of everyday life, lies a carefree beach where a barefoot walk along its sandy shores is almost certain to wash away your worries. The only cost is a lengthy walk down a long stairway and a rather steep hill.

Strands is perhaps the only beach in Orange County with the beauty of a Laguna cove and the thrill of

a San Clemente wave. This beach is stunning at low tide when the sea rolls back leaving behind a thin layer of water reflecting the surrounding headlands.

At higher tides, the waves break crystal clear over a shallow, sandy sea floor giving wave riders a short, but exciting, ride on one of the best-shaped waves in Dana Point.

During calm conditions and a low tide, hike over the southern-most point, across the rocks to a nine foot long rope which will help you scale up and over the ledge to a secluded rocky cove, tide pools, and a tube-shaped sea cave.

SURF REPORT

The Point and Stairs are the two most popular surf breaks at Strands. The Point, located at the south end of the beach, breaks best on a south swell when side waves form over a large rock.

The Stairs, located in between the beach access and the Point, breaks over a large reef. Surfing is best on a medium to high tide.

49

BEACH KEY

Surfing

Tide Pools

Hike Trails

Historic Site

Gift Shop

Visitor Center

Dana Point Cove

BEACH ACCESS: Located along Dana Point Harbor Drive in Dana Point. Take the Pacific Coast Highway to Dana Point Harbor Drive, turn west. After a few miles the road ends at a parking lot. Park in the lot and follow a short stairway to the beach.

BEACH HOURS: 6:00 A.M. - 10:00 P.M.

Dana Point Cove gives visitors a chance to step back in time and experience for themselves the legends of Dana Point. During the 1830's sailors, hired by Boston hide merchants journeyed via Cape Horn and the Strait of Magellan to buy cowhides from the San Juan Capistrano Missionary fathers.

They battled storms, pirates, and occasionally each other in an out-and-out effort to reach the trading shores of Capistrano Bay now known as Dana Point Cove.

Two centuries later, Dana Point Cove has managed to preserve the seafaring spirit of those 19th century mariners. It is especially

interesting for children who can watch sailors aboard the Brig Pilgrim, reenact the daily routines of the 19th century sailor. On this ship, children gong a bell each hour and sing a chant to the hoisting of the sails. Their song rings so clearly that visitors can imagine what it was like when seamen would drop

WARNING!

Dana Point Cove is a Marine Life Refuge. Persons collecting or harming tide pool animals or their environment (including rocks, shells, and water) are subject to a $1,000.00 fine per offense. Please take care to tread lightly and help to preserve this sanctuary for future generations.

Take caution when hiking to the tide pools and sea caves. Visit during low tide only. A high tide can force beachgoers against the cliffs or trap them inside the cave.

their anchor outside the breakers and navigate longboats over enormous swells to the still waters of the bay, waiting there for the missionary fathers to pitch the cowhides from the cliffs.

Today, the rocky intertidal pools with their endless array of sea critters is what brings visitors to Dana Point Cove. To reach the tide pools simply meander along the narrow dirt path flanked by tall headlands on the one side and ocean-drenched fallen boulders on the other. A short hike past the tide pools reveals three sea caves. Legend has it that Spanish pirates hid out at Dana Point Cove and buried their treasure so well, in one of the three caves, that it has yet to be discovered. Whether real or imagined, the true treasure of Dana Point Cove lies in its preserved wildlife and the joy it brings to its visitors.

BEACH KEY

- Lifeguard
- Surfing
- Fishing
- Volleyball
- Bike Trail
- Skate Trail
- Bird Watching
- Park
- Barbecues
- Fire Rings
- Snack Bar
- Beach Rentals
- Camping
- Public Showers
- Restrooms
- Visitor Center
- Parking Fee

Doheny Beach

BEACH ACCESS: Located along Dana Point Harbor Drive and Doheny State Beach in Dana Point. Take the Pacific Coast Highway to Dana Point Harbor Drive, turn west. Turn left into Doheny State Beach.
BEACH HOURS: 6.00 A.M. - 10:00 P.M
CAMPING RESERVATIONS: 800-444-7275

This sixty-two acre beach park, featuring one-hundred-twenty-one camp-sites for overnight camping and one-hundred-seventy picnic sites for day use, is ideal for family weekends, reunions, beach parties and Hawaiian luaus.

Load the car with surfboards, food, and plenty of sunscreen and head down the coast for an active fun-filled weekend of surfing, camping, barbecuing, biking, fishing, bird watching, and much more.

For many regulars this is the place where their love for surfing began. Doheny's familiar, small, slow-rolling waves make it easy to learn how to surf. Protected by the harbor's jetty, the waves are rarely larger than three feet. There is one draw-back however: the water is less clean than most prefer, especially after storms when San Juan Creek is full and it empties into the ocean.

If exploration is more your style, visit the impressive Interpretive Center with its five aquariums,

indoor tide pools, and stuffed
mammals. It is as fascinating as it
is educational. The Doheny State
Beach Interpretive Association also
offers Ranger Campfire Programs
that teach about Marine Ecology
and Oceanography. In addition,
they present an 'annual grunion
night', usually in April, which
features a slide program on marine
animals found in nearby coastal
waters, grunion observation and
discussion followed by a campfire
and marshmallow roast. It's fun!

SURF REPORT

Rivermouth,
Boneyards, First Spot
and Second Spot are
the main surf breaks at
Doheny. This beach
was made famous, in
the 1960's, by surfer
greats who 'danced' on
longboards all the way
to the shore. However,
in the 1970's the Dana
Point harbor was built,
and Doheny's break
went from ten feet high
tubing waves to small,
lazy crumbling lines.
Now the break is
generally good for
beginners and
longboarders. Still, on
occasion, when a
strong south swell
combines with a
northerly offshore
wind, the almost
perfect surf conditions
of the 1960's are
revived with tubing
fast waves that peel to
the shore.

WARNING!

A storm and urban
water runoff drain is
located at the north
end of the beach. The
Orange County
Division of Health
reports that contact
with ponded water,
flowing water, or water
where the runoff
meets the ocean may
cause illness. Swim at
least 100 meters south
of its drainage.

BEACH KEY

- Lifeguard
- Windsurfing
- Swimming
- Kayaking
- Fishing
- Bike Trail
- Park
- Barbecues
- Picnic Tables
- Snack Bar
- Public Showers
- Restrooms

Baby Beach

BEACH ACCESS: Located along Dana Point Harbor Drive in Dana Point. Take the Pacific Coast Highway to Dana Point Harbor Drive, turn west. Continue approximately ¾ of a mile and turn left into the parking lot.
BEACH HOURS: 6:00 A.M. - 10:00 P.M.

Baby Beach boasts a postcard perfect setting with manicured green lawns, shaded picnic tables and ankle high waves that lap gently on shore. It has the sunny appeal of a calm water bay and the ease of a lazy summer afternoon when trees cast shade over napping beachgoers.

As glorious as it is, this beach has one severe problem. The ocean has a variety of pollutants that spoil the bay including sanitary sewer overflow, breakage of underwater sewer pipes, boat discharge, runoff, and wildlife.

Although we discourage swimming here, families can still enjoy on-shore and water craft sport activities. Picnicking, kite-flying, windsurfing, kayaking, and sailing are some of the favored pastimes. Launching non-motorized water craft is a snap and a short paddle or light breeze can bring you outside of the bay in no time.

In addition, a beach-side path perfect for strolling, jogging, and biking leads to many fine cafes and shops. Come to Baby Beach to enjoy the serene setting of a small bay. But for swimming or surfing, try one of the many other clean and beautiful beaches in Orange County.

Capistrano Beach

BEACH ACCESS: Located along the Pacific Coast Highway and Beach Road in Capistrano Beach. Take the Pacific Coast Highway to Beach Road, turn west. Park in the metered parking lot or park free along the highway.
BEACH HOURS: 6:00 A.M. - 10:00 P.M

Trek to the edge of Capistrano Beach to enjoy sand and court sport activities. This easy access beach accommodates active beachgoers while catering to families with small, shore-bound children. Basketball courts, volleyball courts, and a beach-side bike and skate trail make up for this beach's sometimes dangerous and unridable shore-breaking waves.

Other on-shore beach activities include barbecuing at one of many fire rings, kite flying, skipping rocks, and sliding down high-tide sand embankments. Whatever your choice, Capistrano Beach Park offers an active day of on-shore beach fun.

BEACH KEY

- Lifeguard
- Volleyball
- Basketball
- Bike Trail
- Skate Trail
- Beach Rentals
- Public Showers
- Restrooms
- Pay Station

54

SURF REPORT

Capistrano's surf break, Killer Capo, is a solitary peak located in front of the private housing community. It breaks only during low tide on a strong west or strong south swell of ten feet or more.

WARNING!

Capistrano's waves generally break directly on shore and can cause injuries to neck and back. Take caution when swimming here.

San Clemente

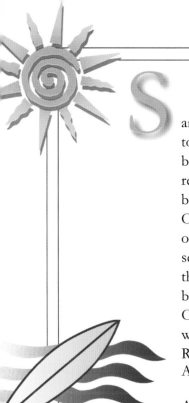

San Clemente, a small and lazy sun-washed beach town, borders some of the best wave riding beaches in California. Each year, tourists and residents flock to San Clemente's famous surf breaks, such as the San Clemente Pier, Trestles, Old Mans, and T-Street to carve up the waves on surfboards, bodyboards and the like. What sets this city apart from other shore towns is that every named beach features waves that break differently from the next. Some like San Onofre and Linda Lane have slow rolling waves, while others like Trestles, State Park, and Riviera have powerful, fast breaking waves. All are tremendously fun.

Avenida Del Mar, a charming 1920's styled street lined with gift boutiques, antique shops, and outdoor cafes, is an excellent place for shopping and dining. Make certain to visit during the first weekend of every month when vendors and farmer's markets set up shop along the promenade.

The Ocean Festival is San Clemente's claim to fame. Each summer, the city sponsors water and sand-sport events where both professional lifeguards and amateur athletes compete in dory boat races, surf contests, swim relays, beach runs, and sand sculpting contests. Art exhibits on surfing and lifeguard legends offer spectators some insight into the surfing lifestyle.

The Fiesta is another exciting San Clemente tradition. The festivities begin with a 5K run and baby stroller race. Come early and experience San Clemente's street party as mariachis and magicians walk along Del Mar Avenue entertaining the crowds. And international food stands, craft booths and amusement park games offer hours of enjoyment. One event not to miss is the salsa challenge where fiery chefs add spicy chili peppers to their secret recipes hoping to earn the reputation for the best salsa north of the border.

Both the Ocean Festival and Fiesta are held in the summer. The days change each year, so it is best to contact the Chamber of Commerce at (949) 492-1131 or the San Clemente Department of Recreation at (949) 361-8264 to inquire about exact dates.

BEACH KEY

Lifeguard

Surfing

Swimming

Bodyboarding

Parking Fee

57

SURF REPORT

The only good reason to visit Poche is the surf. Waves peel right and left over an outside reef and reform to break over an inside reef. Surfing is best on a south swell during a medium to low tide.

WARNING!

A storm and urban water runoff drain is located at the north end of the beach. According to the Orange County Division of Health, contact with the ponded water, flowing water, or water where the runoff meets the ocean may cause illness. Swim at least 100 meters north or south of its drainage.

Poche

BEACH ACCESS: Located along the Pacific Coast Highway and Camino Capistrano in San Clemente. Take the Pacific Coast Highway to Camino Capistrano. Park at the parking meters along the street. The beach access is located directly in front of the Arco gas station. Walk down the stairs, through the tunnel to the beach.

BEACH HOURS: 6:00 A.M. - 10:00 P.M.

There is something unsettling about walking in a dark tunnel, across a rickety deteriorating bridge with thick yellowish-brown liquid stagnating beneath. Some call it sewage, the County of Orange calls it S.W.U.R.P (Storm Water Urban Runoff Pollution), but whatever it is, most everyone will agree, it is offensive. This is the only public access to Poche Beach.

Poche is a small public beach with one redeeming feature: A beach club offering paddleball courts, ping-pong tables, beach rentals and a playground. The only catch is that the club is reserved for Shorecliff residents and their friends. Considering these drawbacks, the reader may question why anyone would come here. The answer is ever the same: The waves.

North Beach

BEACH ACCESS: Located along Avenida Estancion in San Clemente. Take the I-5 freeway to San Clemente and exit Pico, west. Continue two miles to El Camino Real and turn right. Make your first left into the parking lot at Avenida Estancion.
BEACH HOURS: 4:00 A.M. - 12 Midnight

58

North Beach is one of those places that blissfully lingers in your memories long after your visit to the beach.

On summer days, suntanned moms, dads and kids arrive early. They spread out blankets, beach chairs and umbrellas, then dart for the water - their boogie boards, skim boards and floats in tow. Like a large school of fish,

they scramble in and out of tubes, and catch the whitewash, bobbing along together in a could of meringue. Younger children wait for low tide when the waves are still strong enough to get a good ride, but not so strong you fear they will be deposited on a beach in Mexico.

For older kids and parents who find themselves wanting that

ultimate California experience, take a surf lesson from JP's Surf Camp. In no time, JP and his crew will have you surfing like one of the pros.

Boogie boarding and surfing are certain to build up an appetite. Fortunately, Kahuna's Grill, located directly on the strand, serves the best cheeseburgers in town. Enjoy!

59

BEACH KEY

Lifeguard

Swimming

Surfing

Bodyboarding

Fishing

SURF REPORT

Surfing at 204 is good for both novice and experienced surfers. Generally, the waves break slow and mushy, but on a south swell during mid-tide watch out! The waves break fast and hollow, and if you're not prepared, well, they just might swallow you up.

WARNING!

Be cautious of submerged boulders. They are only exposed at low tide, but are always present.

204 Beach

BEACH ACCESS: Located along Buena Vista and Avenida Aragon in San Clemente. From the I-5 freeway exit Pico west. Turn left onto El Camino Real. Continue approximately 1 ¼ miles and then turn right onto Avenida Aragon. Park free along the residential streets. Follow a steep, long stairway to the beach.
BEACH HOURS: 6:00 A.M. - 10:00 P.M.

As the sun rises over a blue-green ocean those fortunate residents of San Clemente, who live in the bluff-top homes overlooking beach 204, peer out of their windows to check the waves. If the breaking billows are great, high, and tubing, it's "go for it time". And many locals begin their day with the lengthy trek down the steep long stairway to the narrow beach.

204 is almost exclusively a surfing beach and is therefore usually less crowded than other San Clemente beaches except during the summer when tourists migrate from North Beach, where surfing is blackballed, to ride the breaks at 204.

During high tide, the shoreline virtually disappears making sunbathing and other on-shore beach activities unfeasible. Often, towels and beach gear must be hoisted onto the boulders which frame the beach to keep them from being washed out to sea. For activities such as smashball, frisbee, and football, it is best to drive or walk north to North Beach where the strand is much wider.

Linda Lane

BEACH ACCESS: Located along Palizada and Seville in San Clemente. Take El Camino Real to Palizada, turn west. Turn right onto Seville. Park in the metered lot and walk through the pedestrian tunnel to the beach.

BEACH HOURS: 6:00 A.M. - 10:00 P.M.

Linda Lane, a narrow beach with gentle waves, is an excellent choice for families with young children. Generally, the waves break small and slow and are tame enough for tots to brave.

In addition, many families enjoy Linda Lane's abundant parking (although it is metered) and its close proximity to the San Clemente Pier, which offers restaurants, snack bars, fishing, and surfing.

And if your children should tire of constructing sand castles and playing in the water, head to the grassy park where play equipment and imagination is likely to keep them occupied for hours.

BEACH KEY

- Lifeguard
- Surfing
- Swimming
- Bodyboarding
- Volleyball
- Park
- Picnic Tables
- Fire Rings
- Restrooms
- Parking Fee

60

SURF REPORT

Linda Lane is part of a long string of beach breaks that arise from the Pier. This thin-lipped, barreling, quick-peaked break is perfect for surfers and bodyboarders wanting to learn tricks, or for anyone who wants to become familiar with the changing conditions of the ocean. Surfing is prohibited 11:00 A.M. - 5:00 P.M., June 15 - September 15.

BEACH KEY

- Lifeguard
- Surfing
- Swimming
- Bodyboarding
- Fishing
- Volleyball
- Barbecues
- Fire Rings
- Restaurants
- Beach Rentals
- Public Showers
- Restrooms
- Parking Fee

SURF REPORT

San Clemente Pier, a popular day and night surfing spot, is a typical beach break with fast short rides that break clean and hollow on a medium-high tide. During higher tides the waves are mushy and better for longboarding.

San Clemente Pier

BEACH ACCESS: Located along Avenida Del Mar in San Clemente. Take El Camino Real to Avenida Del Mar, turn west. Proceed straight approximately 1.5 miles to a metered parking lot. Walk down a gently sloped hill to the beach.

BEACH HOURS: 4:00 A.M. - 12 Midnight

A visit to the San Clemente Pier makes for an action packed day. This lively atmosphere embraces a festive and competitive spirit with city sponsored events such as the Ocean Festival, and Fourth of July firework extravaganza.

The Pier divides the beach into south and north sections. The south end is where families enjoy bodyboarding, swimming, and sand castle building. While the north end is where surfers rule the waves and the beach.

For a volleyball game, head north past the clock tower to what locals call Second Spot. But, be prepared to play against some of the best players in town.

If fishing is more your speed, cast your line off the 1200 foot wooden pier, equipped with bait and tackle shop, benches, and sinks. Catch a large enough fish, and you may even get your picture on the fisherman's board of fame.

And finally, end your day with a tropical drink and sunset dinner at The Fisherman's Restaurant located at the base of the pier.

T-Street Beach

BEACH ACCESS: Located along Trafalgar Lane in San Clemente. Take El Camino Real to Trafalgar Lane, turn west. Park at the parking meters or free along the residential streets. Walk across the bridge and down a steep, but short stairway to the beach.

BEACH HOURS: 6:00 A.M. - 12 Midnight

BEACH KEY

Lifeguard

Surfing

Swimming

Bodyboarding

Skimboarding

Snack Bar

Beach Rentals

Fire Rings

Public Showers

Restrooms

Parking Fee

62

During the summer, this ordinarily quiet beach is brought to life with children's laughter and imagination. The shores are strewn with sand castles, pails, and shovels. And children find camaraderie in chasing the seagulls and jumping the waves.

Surfing, bodysurfing, and bodyboarding are excellent ways to cool off from the summer's heat. The waves are good for beginners as well as experts. However, low tide is the best time for small children, eager to ride bodyboards over cottony foam, to test their courage in ankle high waves that roll gently to shore.

T-Street Beach is one of the most charming beaches in San Clemente, but it is also one of the most popular. It gets very crowded during the summer. So arrive early to secure your place on shore and to enjoy the excellent combination of sun, surf, and family fun.

SURF REPORT

T-Street has fun peaks that break right and left. Surfing is best on a south swell.

From June 15 - September 15, surfers have to dawn patrol or go out for evening sessions because from 11:00 a.m. - 6:00 p.m. surfing is blackballed.

BEACH KEY

Lifeguard

Surfing

Swimming

Bodyboarding

Skimboarding

Sun Bathing

Sand Castle Building

Kite Flying

SURF REPORT

Lost Winds is a typical beach break that pitches barrels during a south swell. It is a fast, short ride, but features less crowded waves than other San Clemente beaches.

Lost Winds

BEACH ACCESS: Located along Calle de los Alamos and Lasuen Street in San Clemente. Take the I-5 freeway to El Camino Real. Turn west onto West Avenida Valencia. Turn left onto Ola Vista. Turn right onto Avenida de los Lobos Marinos. Turn right onto Lausen.
BEACH HOURS: 6:00 A.M. - 10:00 P.M.

On hot summer days, when some of San Clemente's most popular beaches, such as The San Clemente Pier, T-St, and North Beach are bustling with children and tourists, and when finding a parking place is nearly impossible, many San Clemente locals find a solution in Lost Winds Beach. Located along Calle de los Alamos and Lausen Street, this beach's access is so

well hidden that it is generally sparsely populated.

At Lost Winds, not only is the beach strand uncrowded but parking is easy and, as an added attraction, it's free! For those beachgoers who prefer bodyboarding, surfing, and sunbathing to digging for quarters and making a mad dash to the car to prevent a meter

from expiring, then Lost Winds may be just the place for you.

One disadvantage however, is the access is somewhat painful. It involves a hardy walk down a long and somewhat dangerous stairway (there are no hand rails) and then a small descent along a steep dirt path and finally across rail road tracks.

Riviera

BEACH ACCESS: Located along Avenida la Costa in San Clemente. Take the I-5 freeway, exit El Camino Real to Avenida Valencia. Turn left onto South Ola Vista. Turn right onto Avenida de la Riviera. Turn right onto Calle Montecristo. Turn left onto Avenida la Costa. The access is located behind the four palm trees. Walk down an easy stairway to the beach.
BEACH HOURS: 6:00 AM - 10:00 P.M.

A visit to local's favorite, Riviera Beach, gives visitors a chance to experience San Clemente's surfing lifestyle and ever present waves.

Riviera is a wide beach strand with good surfing waves and a devoted population of surfers, who are very reluctant to divulge any information about their secret break. They regard Riviera as their sacred privilege only to be passed on from one San Clemente native to the next.

However, once you have discovered Riviera, you will be graciously welcomed with the expectation that you too will keep this beach a secret, and odds are you will!

BEACH KEY

Lifeguard

Surfing

Swimming

Bodyboarding

Skimboarding

SURF REPORT

Riviera is a fun beach break that takes all kinds of conditions and handles most swells. Directly in front of the access, water run-off pushes sand into the line-up creating sandbars that form A-framed waves suitable for novice and pro surfers. North, south or west swells, Riviera breaks good, but mostly the break is sectiony and changes shape with swell direction. These sections create numerous breaks, which thin out the crowds and offer hollow barrels and racy shoulders.

65

BEACH KEY

Lifeguard

Surfing

Swimming

Bodyboarding

Snack Bar

Beach Rentals

Fire Rings

Public Showers

Restrooms

Parking Fee

SURF REPORT

Calafia has two main surf breaks. The first, located directly in front of the beach access, is hollow, but can also get closed out. In the summer this is a haven for bodyboarders.

The second break, located under the campgrounds, is fast, heavy, and mostly peaky. A strong south swell brings waves that are 6 inches to 1 foot thick, pitching lips that will either glory you in the tube or bury you.

Calafia

BEACH ACCESS: Located along Calafia in San Clemente. From the I-5 freeway south, exit Calafia. Proceed straight through the stop sign. Continue approximately 1 mile. Park in the metered lot and follow the path to the beach. From the I-5 freeway north, exit Magdalena south. Turn right onto Mendocino. Turn left onto Del Presidente. Turn right onto Calafia and follow Calafia to the metered lot. BEACH HOURS: 6:00 A.M. - 10:00 P.M.

Calafia State Beach, directly adjoining San Clemente State Park, is named after a mythical Amazon Queen who, according to legend, fed men and their male offspring to winged lions.

It shares the same beach strand and excellent waves with San Clemente State Park and is a good alternative if you are not camping and do not want to commit to the entrance fee.

Although it has a rugged, almost raw appearance, it still caters to modern tastes with a snack bar and beach rentals.

San Clemente Park

BEACH ACCESS: Located along Califia and San Clemente State Park in San Clemente. From the I-5 freeway south, exit Califia. Proceed straight through the stop sign and turn left into San Clemente State Park. From the I-5 freeway north, exit Magdalena south. Turn right onto Mendocino. Turn left onto Del Presidente. Turn right onto Califia and finally turn left into San Clemente State Park.

BEACH HOURS: 6:00 A.M. - 10:00 P.M.

CAMPING RESERVATIONS: 800-444-7275

BEACH KEY

- Lifeguard
- Surfing
- Swimming
- Bodyboarding
- Camping
- Fire Rings
- Public Showers
- Restrooms
- Visitor Center
- Parking Fee

Providing the ultimate in surfing adventures due to its phenomenal wave break, San Clemente State Park is a surfer's paradise. To reach the beach, follow the steep beach access down one of two poorly paved trails to a mile of soft white strand. If preferred, one can also bike along the ocean view path.

There is another part of the park that is certainly worth mentioning. On the bluffs above the beach are one hundred and sixty scenic campsites. Here those searching for an educational experience can check out the self-guided nature tour, visit the interpretive center or join the Ranger Campfire to learn about Marine Ecology and Oceanography. All of the above for a six dollar entrance fee.

SURF REPORT

At State Park a reef located directly in front of the beach access creates an "A framed" peak that breaks right and produces clean, hollow barrels. It is capable of holding its shape up to 12 feet, but anything bigger than that, forget it! After 12 feet, thick walls of water crash forcefully into a shallow sand bar. Any attempt to take off might drill you into the bottom.

BEACH KEY

- Lifeguard
- Surfing
- Bodyboarding
- Bike Trails
- Hike Trails
- Bird Watching
- Fire Rings

Trestles

BEACH ACCESS: Located along Los Christianitos Road in San Clemente. Take the I-5 freeway to Los Christianitos Road, exit east. Turn left onto El Camino Real. Turn right into Trestles State Beach parking lot. From the parking lot, walk towards the bridge and turn left at the bike trail sign. Follow the long path to the beach.
BEACH HOURS: 6:00 A.M. - 10:00 P.M.

Trestles, labeled the 'Hawaiian pipeline of Southern California' is so named because of its legendary surf. It has a world-renowned reputation for outstanding shaped waves.

Although the surf is enticing, the mile long beach access deters many people, thereby allowing the more serious surfers to enjoy the less crowded waves.

Trestles Beach is a broad stretch of shoreline intersected by the San Mateo Creek. It's worth bringing your binoculars since you will have an opportunity to see many species of birds as well as mammals in their natural wetland habitat. You may even see scrub jays perched atop scrub oak trees, or deer drinking from the creek, or bobcats crossing your path at dusk.

Trestles Beach has an interesting history. It wasn't always in public use. During World War II, President Franklin D. Roosevelt

Cottons, located just north of the beach trail, is a typical reef break that is good on almost any swell. In the 60's and 70's, Cottons was home to big-name surfers. Now, it is an uncrowded forgotten little spot with steep lefts and long waves for experienced longboarders.

Uppers features long walls that break right, over a cobble stone bottom. These fast, high performance, shore breaking waves are best for experienced shortboarders.

South of Uppers, Lowers, another shortboarding wave featuring steep lefts and long rights breaks best on south and southwest swells.

Middles, a fairly consistent wave that breaks both right and left during a west swell, is a small break that is generally not too crowded and is best for longboarders.

Churches is best known for its clean, long breaks. Good in winter, it is one of the best longboarding waves in South Orange County.

dedicated Camp Pendleton as a marine base, virtually cutting off public access to Trestles. However, the surfers found this impossible to accept; they wouldn't give way without a fight. Drawn by the magnetic pull of perfect waves, surfers would often find a way to get past barbed wire, brave the threat of being shot with rock salt, imprisonment, heavy fines, and even surfboard confiscation. This struggle lasted until the Presidency of Richard Nixon. It wasn't until he moved into Casa Pacifica, the Western White House that overlooks Trestles, that public beach access was finally granted. Evidently, President Nixon was moved when he was confronted by a surfer who asked, "Why is the President the only one who is allowed to enjoy the best surf beach in Orange County?" It goes without saying that President Nixon is a hero to most of the surfing community.

69

BEACH KEY

- Lifeguard
- Surfing
- Bodyboarding
- Kayaking
- Fishing
- Volleyball
- Alcohol Allowed
- Dogs Allowed (Restricted Hours)
- Fire Rings
- Public Showers
- Restrooms
- Parking Fee

San Onofre

BEACH ACCESS: Take the I-5 freeway and exit Basilone Road, west. Continue approximately 1.5 miles and turn right at San Onofre Surf Beach.
BEACH HOURS: 6:00 A.M.- 10:00 P.M.
WARNING: San Onofre gets very crowded on summer weekends. You may experience an hour or more wait to get into the beach. To avoid the long wait arrive before 8:00 a.m.

San Onofre Surf Beach is technically considered San Diego County. However, because of its close proximity and enormous popularity among Orange County residents, it deserves its own review.

San Onofe Surf Beach brings visitors back in time to the surf days of Gidget and Moondoggie, where surfers gathered round the barbecue sharing food and swapping stories of the ultimate ride. Here, shrimp and fish still roast over the grill and locals continue to tout the glories of their perfect ride. For many "Sano" regulars, their weekends begin by packing the surfmobile with all the necessary gear - surfboards, wax, beach chairs, sun screen, coolers, and fire-wood- and arriving at daybreak to watch the sun rise as they paddle out into the glassy surf.

There is a legend at San Onofre Surf Beach that surfers here will never grow old. Many locals

claim this beach to be "Peter Pan's Never Never Land", the fanciful island where children stay young forever. After a visit you too just might believe, especially after watching senior citizens catch a perfect right, hang ten then pull a headstand on the inside wave.

Join in all the fun as San Onofre Surf Club sponsors annual events such as authentic Hawaiian luaus, surf contests, volleyball tournaments and much more. Or join the regulars in bocce ball, horse-shoes, or good old fashioned water balloon fights.

SURF REPORT

San Onofre's main surf breaks from north to south are as follows: The Point, Old Man's, Dog Patch, Nukes, and Sirens.

The Point is the first wave break you see as you enter the park. Old timers surf these reliable rights.

On a south swell and offshore wind, Old Man's is the ideal surf break for longboarding. Outside waves break about a quarter of a mile offshore and reform middle and inside peaks.

Dog Patch, just south of Old Man's, is generally an uncrowded peak with easy, slow rolling, mushy waves that are great for beginning surfers.

Nukes, located directly in front of the power plant, breaks long and left over two pipes.

Sirens is a fickle break located just south of the power plant. It features fast and hollow peaks on windless, small swell days.

BEACH KEY

- Lifeguard
- Surfing
- Swimming
- Bodyboarding
- Tent Camping
- Hike Trail
- Bike Trail
- Fire Rings
- Public Showers
- Restrooms
- Parking Fee

SURF REPORT

Locals would like to keep this surf spot a secret. With six paths that lead down to six different surf breaks, consistent, uncrowded waves that break both right and left and clean peeling tubes, Trails is an excellent choice for a day of surfing.

San Onofre, Trails

BEACH ACCESS: Located off Basilone Road in South San Clemente. Take the I-5 freeway to Basilone Road, exit west. Follow the road 3 miles to San Onofre Trails State Beach entrance.
BEACH HOURS: 6:00 A.M. - 10:00 P.M.
CAMPING RESERVATIONS: 800-444-7275

San Onofre Trails feels like 'Coastal California' prior to 20th century development. Large sandstone cliffs, which in the spring are bedecked with purple and gold flowers, give way to three and a half miles of pristine shoreline and turquoise colored waters.

In addition to beautiful beaches, this 300 acre state park features three miles of hiking trails and bike paths plus 221 campsites that were built from the abandoned part of the Old Coast Highway, which are little more than slabs of pavement with a small dirt area where one can pitch a tent.

Although camping accommodations are somewhat rustic, many visitors find it charming and come back year after year. For this reason, it is best to make camping reservations far in advance. And be sure to ask for a blufftop site close to a beach trail.

Afterword

Sun, Sand & Surf, was written from a genuine desire to bring to readers the sense of relief and freedom a visit to the beach can provide. For it is there that you are allowed to shed the clothes, manners and cares of everyday life and behave like a child again: running, swimming, sunbathing and building sandcastles. The sun will inevitably set and the tide will ultimately wash away your footprints, but in the end you will always have your memories of your days at the beach.

We, at *Sun, Sand & Surf,* would be delighted to hear about your experiences at any Orange County beach or any other beach you find noteworthy.
Please send all correspondence to:

Vista Pacifica Publishing Company
E-mail: vistapacifica@usa.com

Sun, Sand & Surf Recommendations

Catalina Passenger Service, Inc.
400 Main Street
Balboa, CA 92661
Phone: (949) 673-5245   (800) 830-7744
Web: www.catalinainfo.com
Travel in style on the Catalina Flyer.
The luxury catamaran features a lounge-type setting with tables, booths, cocktail and snack bar and choice of inside or outdoor seating.

Gondola Company Of Newport Beach
3400 Via Oporto, Suite 103
Newport Beach, CA 92663
Web: www.gondolas.com
For an evening you will never forget!
Love, romance and music. Ride in a Venetian gondola and enjoy the beautiful bay and canals of Newport Beach, California.

Ocean Institute
24200 Dana Point Harbor Drive
Dana Point, Ca 92629
Phone: (949) 496-2274
Web: www.ocean-institute.org
Experience the ocean as you never have before! Join marine biologists in search of local marine life on a wildlife or bioluminescence cruise, blue whale safari or snorkeling adventure.

The Mint Surf Shop
2727 Via Cascidita Ste.G2
San Clemente, Ca 92672
Phone: (949) 366-6777
The Locals' San Clemente hangout.
All Board Sports, Art & Action Sports Outlet. Check out the latest in "Mintage" fashion & art. Surf Lessons available.

The Fermented Grape
31 E. MacArthur Crescent, Suite 105
Santa Ana, Ca. 92707
Phone: (714) 436-0836
Web: www.tfgwine.com
Specializing in fine
wines,champagnes,
custom & ready-to-go
gift baskets and unique gift items. Wine tastings are available.

Pura Vida Day Spa
27134 Paseo Espada, Suite 201
San Juan Capistrano, CA 92675
Phone: (949) 240-2772
Web: www.PuraVidaDaySpa.com
Located in historic San Juan
Capistrano, California, Pura
Vida Day Spa is both
luxurious and affordable. Come in and relax at the Pura Vida Day Spa with a variety of body treatments including facials, wraps, scrub or hot stone therapy.

J.P Surf Camp
Phone: (949) 547-2088
Web: www.jpssurfcamp.com
Located in beautiful San Clemente, California, JP's Surf Camp offers children and adults the opportunity to learn how to surf or sharpen their surfing skills in a small group environment. Private lessons also available.

Dana Point JetSki & Kayak Center
34671 Puerto Place
Dana Point Ca 92629
Phone: (949) 661-4947
Web: www.danapointjetski.com
Kawaski watercraft and Hobie Kayak dealer. Open year round. Hourly rentals of jetski, kayaks & surfboards. Tours also available.

Newport Dunes RV Park
1131 Back Bay Drive
Newport Beach, CA 92660
Reservations: (800) 765-7661
Web: www.newportdunes.com
Situated along the lower portion of the upper bay, vacationers can camp in R.Vs or tents and enjoy sunning on a white sandy beach, sailing or kayaking the bay, swimming in the pool, working on their muscles at the fitness center, dining at the Back Bay Café or watching television in the clubhouse.

73

Davey's Locker Sportfishing, Inc.

400 Main Street
Balboa, CA 92661
Phone: (949) 673-1434
Located in the historic Balboa Pavilion, Davey's Locker offers a variety of fishing trips year round. One half day, three quarter day, full day twilight and shark trips. Equipment, tackle and fishing licence are available at the landing. December through March, whale watching is the premier activity. Trips depart twice daily during the week and three-times-a-day on weekends.

Marina Watersports

600 East Edgewater Avenue
Newport Beach, CA 92661
Phone: (949) 673-3372
Web: www.marinawatersports.com
Newport Bay's largest & most diversified water activity center offers self-guided tours of the bay on your choice of 5 types of electric, power or sail watercraft. Sea-doo jetski rentals, sportfishing in a Boston Whaler & parasailing over the Pacific.

MokiTom Photagraphy

(949)-280-7671
www.mokitom.com
Take the Orange County beaches home with you through the lens of MokiTom! His photography is perfect for home accents or can be used commercially on web sites or as stock photography. Specialties include surfing, marine mammals, exotic birds, and the big waves of Southern California.

Dana Point Youth And Group Facility

34451 Ensenada Place
Dana Point, CA 92629
Phone: (949) 923-2215 or (949) 923-2218
Web: www.ocparks.com/dpyg/
The Dana Point Harbor Youth and Group Facility is a waterfront center overlooking Baby Beach in Dana Point. This outstanding facility is dedicated to the promotion and education of boating, sailing and safety around the water. The one-acre site is the nucleus of many youth and adult programs. The activities encompass everything from basic boating, rowing, canoeing, sailing, marine safety education and ocean themed summer camps. The 8,000 square feet of public buildings are also available for rental and provides an excellent setting for weddings, family gatherings or business conferences.

Cristopher Perry

AT THE MISSION
31770 Camino Capistrano, Suite E
San Juan Capistrano, CA 92675
Phone: (949) 496-0600
Web: www.cpsalon-mission.com
Hit the town with a romantic hair up-do or experiment with hair-cut and color for that hot new look.We are a creative team of execellent hairstylists located in a beautiful and unique design space, located across from the San Juan Mission. Be sure to come in and rejuvenate and relax with a variety of beauty treatments which include spa quality facials, makeup applications and much more. Salon featured on television and voted in top "200 of the Modern Salon Magazine".
Remember, "It's more than just a hair style, it's a life style."

Dana Point Wharf Sportfishing

34675 Golden Lantern
Dana Point, CA 92629
Phone: (949) 496-5794
Web: www.danawharfsportsfishing.com
Offering five to twelve hour fishing trips, sportfishing charters and whale watching cruises (December -March). Gear rentals and sports shop with a wide selection of tackle, rods, reels and sundries.

Hotel Recommendations

The Holiday Inn Costa Mesa
3131 South Bristol Street
Costa Mesa, CA 92626
Phone: (714) 557-3000
Web: www.hicostamesa.com
Winner of the 2001 Renovation of the Year Award (Six Continents Hotels Inc.), the Holiday Inn Costa Mesa is the perfect hotel at the ideal location. The hotel is just minutes from sparkling beaches, amusement parks, sporting events, world-class shopping and John Wayne airport.

Crowne Plaza
17941 Von Karman Avenue
Irvine, CA 92614
Phone: (949) 863-1999
Web: www.irvineca.crownplaza.com/
The award- winning 14-story Crown Plaza Irvine is conveniently located for both the Business and leisure traveler. The perfect base from which to explore Orange County, the hotel is a short drive from Disneyland, Newport & Laguna Beaches, Santa Ana Zoo, and Knotts Berry Farm.

CROWNE PLAZA
IRVINE

The Islands Hotel Newport Beach
690 Newport Center Drive
Newport Beach, CA 92660, USA
Tel: (949) 759-0808
Web: www.theislandhotel.com
The Islands Hotel Newport Beach reflects the vibrant Southern California lifestyle -- combining luxury with a sense of casual elegance and comfort. Newport Beach offers miles of beautiful beaches and an incredible array of shopping, dining, sporting, sightseeing and cultural activities. Many of the spacious guest rooms offer panoramic views from private balconies encompassing either lovely Newport Harbor and the Pacific Ocean, or the pool terrace or Newport Back Bay.

Doryman's Inn
2102 West Ocean Front
Newport Beach CA 92663
Phone: 949.675.7300
Web: www.dorymansinn.com
Romance, Luxury, & resounding elegance, The Doryman's Inn expresses the intrigue of briefly encountering the Glamour of a past era.

Vacation Village
647 South Coast Hwy
Laguna Beach, CA 92651
Phone: (949) 494-8566
Web: www.vacationvillage.com
Located on 300 feet of beach with stunning views of the Pacific coast. The casual style atmosphere of the hotel offers 130 guest rooms, kitchenettes, & suites. A two block walk to art galleries, dinning and shopping.

Casa Laguna Inn
2510 South Coast Highway
Laguna Beach, CA 92651
Phone: (949) 494-2996
Web: www.casalaguna.com
Built in the 1920's as a private residence and used by artists as a reference and vantage point on California's sea coast, Casa Laguna Inn and Spa offers guests casual luxury in a one of a kind setting.

Hotel La Casa del Camino
1289 South Coast Highway
Laguna Beach, CA 92651
Phone: (949) 497-2446
Web: www.casacamino.com
Located at Cress Street Beach! Historic Spanish styled Hotel, built in 1927 as a getaway for the Hollywood crowd. Restaurant & bar on site.

Wood's Canyon Villa Apartments

28520 Wood Canyon Dr.
Aliso Viejo, CA 92656
1-866-239-9151 (Toll Free)
Contemporay hillside living exceeds your high expectations. Overlooking the skyline of Aliso Viejo and Saddleback Valley, Aliso Viejo's prize community, Wood Canyon Villa is nestled amongst a hillside which offers the relaxing atmosphere of serene, open space and soothing ocean breezes. Our apartment homes are designed for those who appreciate spacious, well-designed luxury apartments.

Doubletree:
Guest Suites

34402 Pacific Coast Hwy
Dana Point, CA 92629
Phone: (949) 661-1100
Web: www.doubletreehotels.com
A beautiful California style hotel located directly across from Doheny State Beach. All 196 suites feature a spacious bedroom with french doors to adjoining living area.

Best Western Casa Blanca

1601 North El Camino Real
San Clemente, CA 92672
Phone: (949) 361-1644
Web: www.bwcasablanca.com
Ole Hanson styled Resort just two blocks from North Beach and 204 Beach.

Holiday Inn

111 South Avenida de la Estrella
San Clemente, CA 92672
Phone: 949.361.3000
Email: holidaysc@aol.com
This charming Mediterranean-style resort overlooks the blue Pacific Ocean in the heart of the lovely beach community of San Clemente. Halfway between Los Angeles and San Diego.

Dana Point Marina Inn

24800 Dana Point Harbor Drive
Dana Point, CA 92629
Phone: (949) 496-1203
Overlooking the Dana Point marina and harbor, the hotel offers a fitness center, outdoor pool, business center with a computer, fax, complimentary wireless Internet access & secretarial services.

Blue Lantern Inn

34343 Street of the Blue Lantern
Dana Point, CA 92629
Phone: (949) 661-1304
Web: www.foursisters.com
Situated on the bluff above the Dana Point Yacht Harbor. This award winning Inn Combines Cape Cod feel with the open, airy spaces of Southern California. Rooms feature fireplace, sitting area, oversized bathroom, spa tub and refrigerator.

Casa Tropicana Bed & Breakfast

610 Avenida Victoria
San Clemente, CA 92672
(Across the street from the world famous San Clemente Pier)
Phone: (949) 492-1234
Toll Free: (800) 492-1245
www.casatropicana.com

E-Mail: casatrop@BestOfSanClemente.com
Overlooking the Pacific Ocean, at the San Clemente Pier, the Casa Tropicana holds the promise of adventure, sun, sand and surf. With a five mile stretch of sandy beaches and vast blue ocean, you will feel you are in a secluded tropical paradise. San Clemente's Casa Tropicana is California's answer for that special place to escape for an intimate mini-vacation or to fulfill a fantasy of restful seclusion in a tropical paradise with someone special.

Restaurant Recommendations

Blackie's by the Sea: Bar
2118 West Oceanfront
Newport Beach, CA 92663
Phone: (949) 675-1074
A local tradition since 1951. Known for the coldest beer in Orange County and the best mixed drinks in the city. Blackie's by the sea features pool tables and sports television. Located on the boardwalk at Newport Pier.

The Rib Trader
911 South El Camino Real
San Clemente, CA 92672
Phone: (949) 492-6665
Web: www.ribtraders.com
An outstanding BBQ experience surrounded by local surf memorabilia. Full menu and live music on weekends. Great food and fun.

Fisherman's Restaurant & Bar
611 Avenida Victoria
San Clemente, CA 92672
Phone; (949) 498-6390
Fresh seafood, steaks, oyster bar, breakfast, lunch and Sunday brunch on the San Clemente Pier. Daily happy hour specials with sunset views.

Takao Japanese Restaurant
425 North El Camino Real
San Clemente, CA 92672
Phone: (949) 498-7111
San Clemente's premiere Japanese restaurant and Sushi bar. Enjoy vegetable tempura, teriyaki dishes, fresh sushi and karaoke.

Cassano's Pizza
626 Avenida Victoria
San Clemente, CA 92672
Phone: (949) 361-0522
Located across from the SC Pier. Open-air dining room, delivery, or picnic at the beach. Pizza, salads, pasta, sandwiches, beer and wine.

Iva Lee's
555 North El Camino Real
San Clemente, CA 92672
Phone: (949) 361-2855
Come on in, have a seat and sit a spell in this authentic New Orlean's style restaurant. Enjoy live blues & Creole cuisine.

Renaissance
24701 Del Prado
Dana Point, CA 92629
Web: www.renaissance-danapoint.com
The area's premiere "live music" restaurant with enticing California cuisine, extensive wine list, full bar and patio with fireplace.

The BeachFire Bar & Grill
204 Avenida Del Mar Suite D
San Clemente, CA 92672
Phone: (949) 366-3232
Web: www. BeachFireBarandGrill.com
BeachFire celebrates California's coastal lifestyle with killer, live music and a great menu of grilled fish, steaks, ribs, tacos, Sunday brunch, and full bar. This restaurant has all the ingredients for a great time.

Kahuna's Grill At North Beach
1700 Avenida Estancion
San Clemente, CA 92672
Phone: (949) 395-2878
E-mail: Kahunagrill@yahoo.com
Situated directly on the sand at North Beach, enjoy San Clemente's best burger while watching the dolphins swim just offshore. Open May - September. Private parties, luaus and catering available.

Carbonara's Trattoria Italiana
111 Avenida Del Mar
San Clemente, CA 92672
Phone: (949) 366-1040
Web: www.carbonara.com
Authentic Northern and Southern Italian cuisine. Family owned and operated. Fresh bread and deserts made daily.

Order Form

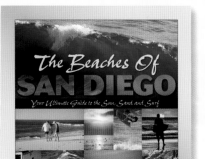

SUN, SAND & SURF
The Ultimate Guide To Orange County Beaches

Quantity	Book Price	Shipping & Handling	Subtotal
	$27.50	$6.00	
California residents please add 7.75% sales tax per book.			
Total			

The Beaches of **SAN DIEGO**
Your Ultimate Guide to the Sun, Sand and Surf

Quantity	Book Price	Shipping & Handling	Subtotal
	$29.50	$6.00	
California residents please add 7.75% sales tax per book.			
Total			

Santa Barbara County Beaches

Quantity	Book Price	Shipping & Handling	Subtotal
	$27.50	$6.00	
California residents please add 7.75% sales tax per book.			
Total			

TEMECULA WINE COUNTRY

Quantity	Book Price	Shipping & Handling	Subtotal
	$27.50	$6.00	
California residents please add 7.75% sales tax per book.			
Total			

Please send check or money order to:
Vista Pacifica Publishing Company
P.O. Box 373 • Dana Point, CA 92629-0373
Telephone: (949) 395-2878 • E-mail: Vistapacifica@usa.com

Sun, Sand & Surf Index

Board Rental

REEDEMABLE FOR ONE COMPLIMENTARY

Compliments of Vista Pacifica Publishing Company and Kuhuna's Grill At North Beach. This certificate is redeemable for one complimentary board rental when the bearer buys the first rental at regular price. Please see reverse side for valid requirements and restrictions.

Located on the sand at North Beach in San Clemente.
For reservatations call (949) 395-2878

Void if electronically copied, scanned, or altered

Redeemable For One Complimentary Surf Lesson

JP'S SURF CAMP

Redeemable for one complimentary hour surf lesson when the bearer buys the first hour lesson at regular price. Compliments of Vista Pacifica Publishing Company and JP'S Surf Camp. Please see reverse side for valid requirements and restrictions.

For reservatations call (949) 547-2088
or visit our website at www.jpssurfcamp.com

oid if electronically copied, scanned, or altered

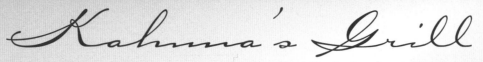

Kahuna's Grill

This section should be completed by Kahuna's Grill At North Beach when the certificate is redeemed. Mail completed certificate to: Vista Pacifica Publishing Company, P.O. Box 373, Dana Point, CA 92629-0373

Name of Guest

Guest Home Address

Guest City   State   Zip

Guest Home Telephone Number

Signature

Certificate is good for one complimentary board rental with the purchase of one rental at the regular price. Offer valid May through September. Subject to availability. Advanced reservations recommended. Restrictions apply. Vista Pacifica Publishing Company is not responsible for any changes in individual rental operation or policy. By use of this certificate, consumer agrees to release Vista Pacifica Publishing Company from any liability in connection with their travel to and rental with Kahuna's Grill. This certificate may not be reproduced and cannot be used in conjunction with any other promotional offers. Certificate must be redeemed at Kahuna's Grill by December 31, 2007. Void where prohibited. Void if electronically copied, scanned or altered. Certificate expires December 31, 2007.

JP'S SURF CAMP

This section should be completed by JP'S Surf Camp when the certificate is redeemed. Mail completed certificate to: Vista Pacifica Publishing Company, P.O. Box 373, Dana Point, CA 92629-0373

Name of Guest

Guest Home Address

Guest City   State   Zip

Guest Home Telephone Number

Signature

Certificate is good for one complimentary hour surf lesson with the purchase of one-hour lesson at the regular price. Offer valid May through September. Subject to availability. Advanced reservations recommended. Restrictions apply. Vista Pacifica Publishing Company is not responsible for any changes in individual surf camp operation or policy. By use of this certificate, consumer agrees to release Vista Pacifica Publishing Company from any liability in connection with their travel to and surfing with JP'S Surf Camp. This certificate may not be reproduced and cannot be used in conjunction with any other promotional offers. Certificate must be redeemed at JP'S Surf Camp by December 31, 2007. Void where prohibited. Void if electronically copied, scanned or altered. Certificate expires December 31, 2007.